WomensWords

THE OTHER WOMAN: A POETIC PERSONA

Edited by

Rebecca Mee

First published in Great Britain in 2001 by
WOMENSWORDS
Remus House, Coltsfoot Drive,
Peterborough, PE2 9JX
Telephone (01733) 898101
Fax (01733) 313524

HB ISBN 0 75432 545 8
SB ISBN 0 75432 546 6

FOREWORD

Although we are a nation of poetry writers we are accused of not reading poetry and not buying poetry books: after many years of listening to the incessant gripes of poetry publishers, I can only assume that the books they publish, in general, are books that most people do not want to read.

Poetry should not be obscure, introverted, and as cryptic as a crossword puzzle: it is the poet's duty to reach out and embrace the world.

The world owes the poet nothing and we should not be expected to dig and delve into a rambling discourse searching for some inner meaning.

The reason we write poetry (and almost all of us do) is because we want to communicate: an ideal; an idea; or a specific feeling. Poetry is as essential in communication, as a letter; a radio; a telephone, and the main criteria for selecting the poems in this anthology is very simple: they communicate.

CONTENTS

BANKERS

We wear cotton
crushed by the flat heat, or the iron,
and slacks that starch our female figures.

Row, desk,
paper, woman.
Out slip
in slip.

Our wrists flick through the credits
and hotly at the keys, we finger numerals
with manicure precision.

A gaggle of whores
legs spread, for numbers
sheer in amount

Last spring we made confetti
in the bureaux de change, from old currency,
then hid it in the strong room
beneath a crate of cheques.

A harem of nurses
dressed in and dressing
an infected wound.

Once, a manager in royal blue chintz
spat a visit on our in-trays.
It landed, curling the papers below,
upwards as they yellowed.

A doe-eyed bunch
of underclass, spoken to in doggerel,
useless.

Kate North

DEAR MARIA

I was neither your enemy
Nor your friend.
I watched you from afar,
As you laughed and flirted,
Brown hair flying.
With my best mate.
You took your own life,
Not two nights ago,
And the life of the child
That was growing inside you.
Why?
I held your boyfriend,
Shaking in my arms
As I watched the paramedics,
Carry you away,
While blood mingled with tears.
I am angry,
With you and with life.
I reach out to God,
And I do not feel his presence,
But I will never forget,
For every time I close my eyes,
I feel your boyfriend shaking against me,
And blood mingling with tears.

Karen McKee (13)

END OF THE AFFAIR

What is he doing here?
I told him it's over.
Our relationship has become
a habit I must escape from.
And still he comes back,
the sad sheep eyes
saying he can't go on.
He can't sleep, he can't eat.
Who will look after him?
I am not his mother.

Cold, he says I am
Cold and cruel as the moon
shining in at the window.
I wish I was.
I could tell him to
get the hell out of my life.
I prevaricate,
words don't say what I mean.
I stumble,
trying to save him
And destroy us both.

Kate Murphy

TAKEAWAY

I used to like Chinese food
But you
You put me right off it
The way you said
'Cantonese'
with that look in your eyes
which made me feel I was to blame

Each slice of meat
Was part of me
Neat packets of rice
Flattened
And patted
To fit in nice

It won't be the same again
For me

Licking your fingers
You think you can choose
Call numbers like scores
I suppose that's all you know

But do you know how it feels
To be eaten alive?
Unable to stop
The crawling
And gnawing inside
Scared
And angry
Angry that you're scared
Being oh so slowly sliced

And the gutter papers lie
The TV talks to itself
And no one really listens at all

And the thing that gets me most
Is you think you're being *nice*
And sociable
And I should be pleased
At being squeezed
And not rejected by you

And I hate you
Because now I can never forget
Your choice

You've wormed into my head
Without asking what I thought
Changed it
Like this week's special

I would have chosen
to go on enjoying
sweet and sour
but you took away from me the power
to make that choice
with a tin of beef
and black bean sauce
and special fried rice

And by being 'nice'

Diana Clark

THEY CALLED IT BABY BLUES

I once knew a woman
Who was a tape recorder,
Broken and rat infested.

Messages went round endlessly.
'Don't do that. Eat your food.
Don't tease your brother,'
Repeatedly.

She had four little children,
And a faithless husband,
And an upstairs flat,
With elderly neighbours, whispering.

Her doctor sectioned her -
In a word declaring her unfit
To care for her children or herself.
Her children were 'in care',
Her husband in bed,
Her neighbours relieved.

For she was an unfit mother
Who was a tape recorder
Broken and rat infested.
I once knew that woman.

Ann Harrison

YOU MAKE ME SMILE

A lingering smile -
Gleaming eye?
My face illuminates.
Yours?

As I took you in the bath tonight
Between the leaves of verse,
Water caressed the mind
Duplicating hands
That had previously explored.

Receiver sublime.

B J Norris

TIREDNESS

I need sleep.
My whole being calls me to it,
But the floor is covered with toys,
The sink is full of cups and plates,
The laundry box is overflowing.
I don't care.
Just a few minutes rest will revive me.
I haul myself upstairs to bed,
I wriggle around a bit, can't settle,
Then slowly, deliciously, begin to drift away . . .

The baby's crying!

Maybe she'll go off again.

It's getting louder!

She needs me, I must go to her.
I drag myself up, just ten minutes
Since I lay down,
I gently pick up the child, feed her,
Cuddle her, settle her,
Then trudge downstairs with exhausted resignation
To the toys, the cups and the washing
Rather than lying and waiting
For the next cry.
My helpless babe, I would do anything
To protect you, care for you,
And as I stand at the sink I hate myself
For the tiny seed of resentment
Which is swirling round within me amid all the love
Because you now sleep and I cannot.
I am just so tired.

Catherine Champion

WAR VICTIM

She stood in line with her mother and sisters.
The border crossing was in sight, freedom?
They were cold, hungry, and had walked far
An unknown fear, shuddered through the bedraggled,
Line of women, they were dragging girls away.
She hid behind her mother, safe and close
A jeering group approached, they grabbed her
Screaming for her mother, for her sisters,
For her life, as she had known it, so good
They ripped her clothes, her body so special
No man had gazed upon, with eyes or thoughts
Was broken into savagely, not with love, but hate.
She lay there dirty, forlorn no life left,
To look forward to, just total rejection
Death would have been sweeter.

Rosemary Rutherford

UNTITLED

When I am old and have ceased to care,
    What people say and think,
I shall do what I have always wanted to do
    And wear a hat of shocking-pink

I shall go to the children's playground
    And whoop down the highest slide
And laugh at the folk who stand and stare
    And say I should be locked 'inside'

I shall visit the shopping centre
    And behave like a silly clown
And gallop up the escalator
    On the side that is going down

I shall sit in the square with my hat at my feet
    And put on a senseless grin,
And hope that all the passers-by
    Will drop their spare change in

And when my grandchildren come to stay
    I shall tell them how good I've been
We shall go for a walk across the fields
    And paddle in the stream

I shall tell them about my childhood
    The days of yesteryear
And all the happy memories
    The ones I hold most dear

When school was for sitting quietly
    And learning the three Rs
And spelling was a weekly test
    For earning us some stars

My hair is grey and I've lost my waist
   And my belt has nowhere to go
But my spirit's still there, I can sing,
   Three cheers and a ho! Ho! Ho!

Jean Parkhurst

DEMANDS FROM MEN

Where's a pen
And then
What's for tea?
And
A general need
For urgent speed
To just hold this for me
And
Have you seen the car key?
And
Discovers horror shock
There *really is no* matching sock
And
His shirt has not seen an iron
And
Asks puzzled - Why are you cryin'?
And
Guesses from your demeanour
His best suit's still at the cleaners
And worse
It dawns all of a sudden
That there is nowt for pudding!

Megan Mcdonald

GOODBYE TO MR NOBODY

A body in a shallow grave is shortly forgotten
By the people who called themselves friends.
No one can afford, or even cares enough
To give this man a decent burial.
Who will pay the costs or arrange the headstone?
Not any of the hypocrites standing in black,
Drink was the cause of his loss
Encouraged by the wife that was never really his,
(Although the type of girl who was everybody else's).
His dream was only to be happy
To better himself from the gutter where he rose.
The only hope he had was history with the first better offer.
Everything left the day she did
And the only consolation was found
At the bottom of a spirit bottle.
Drank slowly from within a brown paper bag,
He sat in a shop doorway late one night
And forgot his pain forever.
He still sat there cold and alone
Found by a policeman on his beat that evening.
Chillingly, the day his body was submitted to a better life
His wife began to cry.
Not sorry for her actions but relieved to be free.
An unfitting goodbye to a pathetic but forgiving man.

C Miles

THE CREAM BLOUSE

Her legs ached as she grasped the steaming iron.
Wearily, she pushed away a wisp of her tangled brown hair.
Her tired eyes peered through the rain-spotted window,
Seeking comfort from the twinkling orange lights
In the dank, black, night sky.

Handling the slim, cream blouse tenderly,
Her thoughts shifted to her newly-teenaged daughter
Sleeping peacefully in the poster-strewn room above.
Her precious child; once a babe;
Now flowering into the beauty of youth.

She paused in her toil, her work-worn fingers
Instinctively pressing the button of her personal stereo.
Defying the silence of the night, the easy instrumental rhythms
Soothed her soul and comforted her mind.

With renewed energy, she smoothed the creases
In the long, simple sleeves,
Symbolically obliterating the problems of her life.

Her task completed, she laid aside the iron and smiled.
Gently, she pressed the warm cream blouse to her face,
Her love flowing through its crisp folds.
Life was hard - but she was calm.
She knew she and her child would survive.

Sue Wensley

THE PARTING

The years together have melted away
        as though they had never been;
Heady passion of wedded bliss had been replaced
        by a deep and lasting love, companionship.
Perfect knowledge of each other had entwined their hearts
        like the branches of a gnarled old oak.

A large storm brewed over the horizon,
        winds of change gathering momentum.
Lightening struck the tree, shredding it
        into a thousand pieces,
        tearing up the roots of their life together.
He turned, and walked away without a backward
        glance,
uncaring of the hurt and pain he had caused

Grief like a knife thrusts deep into the heart spreading
  until it consumes the whole body,
the very soul.
The body aches and longs for oblivion,
        for inner calm and total peace.
Each new dawn brings further torment
            a realisation of finality.

Hidden amongst the carnage,
unnoticed,
lies a tiny acorn
unblackened it nestles amongst the utter confusion.
A new tree will grow in time, its branches stretching
        upwards and outwards towards the sun.
Time now to take stock, to face whatever lies ahead.
Move into the light, feel the warmth, be unafraid,
be free,
the future beckons.

Joanna Ellen Smith

THE VICTIM

As I lie on my bed I think of yesteryear,
The heartbreak and the sorrow
The beatings and the horror.
At night I'd lie awake in dread
Not knowing what might lie ahead.

To speak, or not to say a word
For all my feelings went unheard.
For all his words were law it's true
Or else you'd end up black and blue.
You slaved all day to make a home
You would not dare to ever roam,
You work your fingers to the bone
For what, violence in the home.

The only time it ever ceased, was when
his lordship lay in a drunken sleep,
I'd lie awake with murder on my mind,
scared to even think of such a crime.
With all my heart I hated this man
I wanted out I couldn't understand.

I had to get out before he put me in
my grave,
For my home was my prison my sanity
I must save,
For the scars I shall carry with me,
Till I'm lying in my grave.

Jean Pringle

LIFE'S BLOOD

Slow, slowly, slowly, stabbing at my loving contained world.
Scrape, scrape, scraping, picking easing the cold steel in,
Lifting the bark slicing the blade through, careless of what you do.
Pain, pain, tug, tug, tugging as the strip is slowly lifted and
                                                              peeled away.
Raw nerves sinewy hidden private depths laid stark to the world.
The blade tugs, rips and strips again.
Pain surging through heart and head.
Pain you never knew the depth of.
Mocking you with each ripping strip.
Your core is laid bare; life is ebbing from your world.
He is with closed eyes, he sees but does not see.
He works dogmatically lifting and stripping.
Casting aside wife, child, friend and home.
Loves blood screams, screaming, pleading, pouring from her soul.

Zoë Rolph

REALITY WINS

My heart felt a long painful knife enter . . . and stay,
Numbness, despair and piercing pain deludes the
silence, discreet silence which emerges within.
I was bleeding and torn, torn into shreds,
I looked down it was only the passion in my heart dying
I will somehow survive, I must cope with this
loneliness, unshared naked loneliness,
How dare these feelings reveal my subconscious state of mind
I feel exposed, rejected and . . . abused.

Dreams come from the skies and fall like rays of sun
and dance upon the erotic mind . . .
Reality, like the violent sea against the rocks
hits hard and crushes the hypothalamus shattering
the senses . . . and hurts.
In fantasy the pain is always pleasure and hurt is
dissolved, assimilated and contained.
How can reality be so cruel and why does it hurt so much
Chemical reactions within have reduced my heart to an atom
protons and neutrons react but do not bond.

Once I felt intense euphoria, excitement, happiness and
deep, deep emotion,
Naive and child-like I could perceive no end . . .
The strong passionate feelings then ultimate utopia,
this to me was infinite . . .
But paradise did not last . . .
Reality wins.

Maureen Rose

BATTERED DREAMS

How long can you wait?
Ever hopeful, one day it'll be
Your turn
You can lie to others
But never to yourself
It's taken me half a lifetime
To realise that!
How long can you wait?
Searching for that special one
Do they exist?
The one who'll love you always
Put you down never
Make your soul sing so very
Loudly
Who'll pick you up when
You're down
Who'll always be there to love
Want and cherish you
To be the other half of your
Being
Perhaps my vision is to clear!
Battered dreams!

Roberta J Scott

A WELCOME RELIEF

Take all my beds and all of my clothes
and leave me naked and cold.
Whip me and burn me and rape me at will,
But please don't let me grow old.
Take all my friends and all of my hopes.
and shred them before my eyes.
Rip out my heart and place it in view
for all to see my cries.
My loss is so great, my despair so intense
I have lost sense of inhibition,
I cannot hide this pain so fierce,
I can offer no imitation.
My mind is pure trauma in psychological form
My soul has been stolen by an unnatural storm.
Pull out my toe nails and file down my teeth,
Please take my scalp for a sense of relief.
Burn down my house and take all my kin
deprive me of water and tease me with gin.
Laugh at my misery and mock every tear
Shit in my mouth and piss in my ear.
Violate my body, for I no longer care,
My worthless existence refuses repair.
I once had a life full of hope and of dreams
I once had a soulmate to share all of these things.
I once had a family but not any more
Fragmented and shattered
and wrecked to the core.

Julie Fox

SMILE

All those faces looking glum
How sad our youngsters have become
They don't look happy anymore
As search for love involves a score

From drug to drug they cannot see
What they will lose through taking 'E'
And is it worth the risk or cost
As memories fade and lives are lost

We oldies weren't saints you know
We drank too much and some took blow
But most of us remember well
The guys we loved - their looks - their smell

Will they remember when they're old
The lyrics from a song once told

I can't imagine how I'd feel
If all my youth remained unreal
My first true love - the joy and pain
Are firmly planted in my brain

But this was life and this was me
Each weekend joy a memory
And one that's still with me today
As I grow old unfit and grey

But when I see your empty eyes
I wonder if it's worth the lies
Your beauty fading through abuse
As you become a sad recluse

Think on - be brave - believe in you
Life can be good if you want it to
Let's see a smile and one that's real
Reflecting how you *really feel*

Evelyn McCormick

WASTED YEARS

She looks at him with such disdain
That grows upon her face
She hates with a mighty loathing
That scarcely knows its place
She blames him for her wasted years
She hates 'til she is cold
She despises him for taking her life
And leaving her broken and old

She has heavy heart for the smiling face
That she once knew of old
She longs to caress the body
Of that lover she did hold
She cries at night for him
For the love that did evolve
And is angry that she let him go
Because of her lack of resolve

She looks at him with such regret
And sighs a heavy sigh
She feels no awesome pang of guilt
For the reasons he might die
She just throws her head to the back of the chair
And curses his retirement
And prays to God that some day soon
She will be blessed with his internment

Terri Tibbetts

IT'S MY OWN 'HOME SWEET HOME'

A terraced town house us newly-weds sought
'updating required' - so we brought.

The owner's past were extremely kind,
they left some furniture of theirs behind.
A grease-ridden cooker plus various fixtures,
Rusty and dusty, a real junk yard mixture.

To move in, clearing out had to be done,
I searched in vain for Steptoe and Son.
Amongst the chaos my family did call,
Quite unimpressed by what they saw.

'When will you Hoover?' big brother cried.
'When I possess one,' I replied
'Muck by sunset' was the reference made
to the painted walls of brownish shades.

The jibes flew round, not really unkind,
I was proud of my home, I did not mind.
I dreamt of making everything proper,
I dreamt of owning the brightest knocker.

I wanted a show home, I wanted the best,
It's my own 'home sweet home' - *yah boo to the rest!*

Tracey Morgan

ID

It's different now
Most of the time you're allowed to be you
Least that's what they say
Most people couldn't care. Some people say
That I'm a scrubber
No I'm not
I just don't fork out loads for my clothes
No one notices anyway
It doesn't make me less of a person
Because I don't conform to the ideal society
What's that anyway?
I do what I want, if people don't like it
So what! I'm not living my life for them
I'm like me, I laugh, I cry, I eat
Drink and sleep.
Those are things that we all do.
We do them to survive
So what else matters?

Hannah Shooter

NEW BEGINNINGS

In 1978, after 24 years of 'togetherness',
greener pastures beckoned and my husband was gone.
I was forced to make a fresh start
as a 'single Mum' to our three young children -
living disbelief and humiliation twenty-four
hours of every unwanted day, and yet, somehow,
gaining reassurance from their presumptiveness
and optimism . . .

Even so, recognition and acceptance of my new status was
an unbelievably slow process.

Now the century is turning and it's time for
another new beginning, since
the last of my three children has 'cut the umbilical',
closing the circle on my marriage experience.

Now I am *me*. My experiences have proved to be a
'being and a becoming' - and I'm *here!* - eager for
each new day.

(His 'green pastures', incidentally, turned brown . . .
Mine deepened into a lushness where I wallow in contentment
and greet each beautiful new dawn).

Edna Sparkes

UNTITLED

Butterfly, butterfly,
Your gentle beauty reminds me . . .
Of a new mother kissing her babe,
Of a sucking calf . . .
A child laughing,
A sweet-smelling flower,
A warm summer,
A breath of fresh air which caresses my temper.

Butterfly, butterfly . . .
You have magic.
Magic me!

Heather McCready

THE CLOCK

Our way of Life,
Our ever reliable leader
The keeper of history,
The mark of the moment
The symbol of the future.

It has no passion,
No requests.
Not affected by emotion,
Not controlled by man.
Not judgmental or bitter.

Remaining forever, never changing.
Loved and loathed.
The hope of many,
The despair of others.
When it stops, so do we.

Christine Stevenson (16)

LET'S MAKE A DIFFERENCE

Save the world
Let's make a change
Save it for the children
Make the world a better place
Here is your chance to enjoy life
Let's work together
Make a difference
Let's do what we can
Life should not be a race
We enjoy life whilst others suffer
There is a pleasure to be found
Look at the earth around us
Do not put labels on those you don't know
Look at the world we live in
People see things in different ways
Let that not give us the right to disrespect them
Let everyone be valued equally
Do not let a poor man be judged by his appearance
Let him be judged by his true character
The future is in our hands
Make a decision.

Lauren Morales

CARRICKFERGUS CASTLE

My footsteps seemed to echo
as high as the clouds.
The wind pushes the clouds forward,
hiding the moon's face.

Still as a statue
yet my shadow moves.
It circled me like
a violent tornado.

A silvery white figure like a ghost replaced my shadow.
And with a gasp
I woke up breathless in my bed.

Rebbekkah Murphy (12)

PEACE IN OUR WORLD

I am one person
One person can make a big difference
For us to regain *peace*

All we need is one person
For us all to follow.

In the world we do not have much *peace*
Many countries are in war
And many don't have enough food
But we have more than enough
And do not share enough of what we've got
I think we are greedy
And should share out more

That is my view of *peace.*

Taryn Murray

MY POEM

She sits so peacefully
Listening to the sound of the waterfall,
Gently trickling down into the pool.
The heat of the sun beating down on her body,
Makes her long for the coolness of the pool beside her.
She thinks how lucky she is to be here,
In a peaceful, first-class, American hotel.
She lies with nothing to worry about,
She knows she doesn't want this holiday to end.

Frankie Narayan

DREAMS COME TRUE

Dreams come true
Ambition's never wasted
Chances are everywhere
Just let the light in.
Dreams come true,
People are always there
We all have a protector
Who will always care.
Dreams come true,
Down the tunnel of life
Never alone, if not for yourself
New light from your eyes
More warmth from the sun, just remember this
Everyone has someone.
Whether to guide or to seek
To lead or to follow
Open your heart today
And embrace tomorrow.
Take a deep breath,
Relax and feel safe
Because life is for living
Don't put it to waste.
Dreams come true,
And the light never leaves
My protector always beside me,
My ambitions will be fulfilled.

Hollie Steele (16)

GROWING PAINS

We are brought into the world
All sweet and innocent.
We don't have a say in what
Is said and done.

Then come the dreaded teens
Drink, drugs, smoking and sex.
Our parents and teachers have told us all about them
But some don't listen.
Some think they know better.

'These are the best days of your lives'
My parents say.
But are they really?
I'm soon to find out.

Jennifer McCully

PEACE

Our lives are overcome with rage and fear,
With the need for power and the lust of knowledge.
We must stop living these lives and begin new ones,
For if we don't, a new era cannot be born.
Our souls need to shine with the light of peace,
Not the gloom of darkness.

Darkness which is made of fear, rage, anger.
All the emotions which we have brought on ourselves.
We need to stop living in this darkness,
Inside it we only care for ourselves.
We don't care for those who need us,
For those who make an effort to overcome the rage
And bring on the peace.

We can make ourselves rich and famous,
So that everybody loves us, wants to be us.
Is someone who helps and cares for others
Not more special than a supermodel or pop star?
They are in God's eyes.

For in those eyes there is a dream of peace.
Where every man and woman loves their neighbour,
There is no tension only love.

Are we so clever we think we can
Make peace out of money and power?
We can't, it is these things that have caused the conflict,
Made the wars, killed the people.

God wants us to make an effort,
To do this, we must love each other, look after one another.
Make God's dream come true.

For after all,
There is always light at the end of a tunnel,
Not everlasting darkness. One day, peace will prevail,
And light will shine again.

Emma Parker

MY REFLECTION
(Written for a friend in a time of need)

Look. Open your eyes. Perceive from all angles.
Every ray of light piercing through.
A glance here, a look there,
Or wherever it comes from.
A friendly smile, an empty stare.
All reflected in me. They take
Their role, I follow on.
My reflection in them.
A mutter whispered, a look in a direction.
Hoping they know I'm with them,
Feeling the same.

Their reflection shown in me.
I pray they know,
That a mirror is one thing,
But a friend's eyes reflect onto
You more than you can imagine.
You feel happy and I am ecstatic,
A glint of fear and I'm trembling.
A tear to shed and I am your shoulder.
A moment lost and I am devastated.
I look at you and know,
I'm a reflection of you.

Grace Stirling

STAY

Stay, don't leave and go
Don't leave me here in this awful place
Please don't let me get so low
Tears are streaming, staining my soft, cold face.

You don't seem to understand
How my life is dependant on yours
You need to forever hold my hand
Whilst my love for you continually pours.

The pain in my heart is so acute
I can't hide it, my eyes are too sad
My mind cannot think, I am mute
Please don't leave, stay: please Dad.

Those little things you do every day
The light you bring into the world
The only thing I ask of you is, stay
Don't leave your little girl.

You seem so able and confident
That everything will be okay
Your love for me meant
Your life must turn and go a different way.

So Father all I ask of you
Is stay with life to give
And grant my only wish please do
The wish for you to live.

Hannah Vincent (16)

PARENTS

They are always there calling after us wherever we are,
'Do this . . . do that . . . tidy here . . . tidy there . . .'
What are we their slaves?
Until we are eighteen we are theirs,
Like a jail sentence, imprisoned.
A puppet while they pull the strings.

They seem to think this is good for us.
I think they just like to be mean.
How dare we have fun without them?
Without them . . .
What would we do? No screaming, no puppeteers.
We'd be a puppet without strings.
A jail without bars.
A child however young or old without love.
We'd be nothing, a tumbleweed blown in the wind.
However much we hate to admit it we need them.
Mum, Dad I need you, to be my puppeteers,
So I don't make too many mistakes.

Jenny McKay (13)

DIFFERENCES

Walking down the lonely highway of life,
My only friend is my conscience, some friend.
I march to the beat of racial insults, hurled from side to side.
We, a mysterious people, also have pride.

What does our skin colour matter?
Why do men look only skin deep?
It's what's inside that really matters,
We have feelings too, you know.

Your guns and bombs have so much power.
You have a choice to make.
Yet why do you insist on using them
To harm, not help us? We who feel the pain.

I live forever in a bleak world of fear.
Death surrounds me and swallows me whole.
There is enough evil in this world without adding to it.
We fear illness as much as you do.

If we're tired, we sleep. If we're sad we cry.
If you tell a joke, we laugh. If you poison us, we die.
When it all boils down, there's no difference at all.
Yes, my skin is different, but inside we're all the same;
Afraid, frightened, small.

Sarah McVeigh

CORFE - THE MAJESTIC RUIN

Mist surrounds the century aged stones,
Enveloping, rising up and through the crumbling walls.
Beautiful in the slivers of sunlight.
Picking out dancing shadows,
Somehow a haunting beauty emerges.
Mysteries and dramas could be hidden
Deep in the history around.

White smoke billows out,
As from an old man's pipe it curls.
Wandering around and billowing in the wind,
Wisps of light, white fluffiness in its wake.

The peaceful tranquillity
Seems so loud in its quietness.
Only birdsong, rustling wind in the trees.
As you strain to hear movements,
Sounds of the countryside,
A shrill whistle breaks into the stillness.

The chug of the engine can be faintly heard,
As the path of winding smoke disappears.
The stillness of the magical, misty monument
Stands tall and proud.
Waiting for a glorious day of splendour once again!

Joanne Lewis

THE CITY

The rooftops glittering in the moonlight
The concrete walls, the shop windows, brightly lit
A couple, kissing under a lamppost
A heap of papers rustling in the wind
Dark alleys, screaming car wheels, sirens in the distance
The distance is endless in the city
At night, under the bright moon
During the day, in gleaming sunlight
When hundreds of shadows are rushing past
To work, to live, to be
How do they manage, to kiss, under the lamppost
Across that distance?

Sandra Barkhof

My Father's House

My Father's house has many rooms
It says so in the Bible
The people say you'll feel safe there
I'll have them up for libel

He held me on the mantelpiece
To stop me so from falling
I've never much liked heights since then
And silent screams aren't calling

When you say 'It makes you sick'
You have no comprehension
The sickness took me every night
There never was redemption

Recurring dreams
Recurring screams
The night is darker than it seems
Little star o' shining bright
You didn't help me in the night

The runners ran each on their track
There was no chance of going back
Paralysed, a child of fear
I knew that if they hit the rocks
The light would ne'er draw near

My Father's house has many rooms
And fear has many levels
But the fear that visits every night
Is the worst of all the devils

Lynne Luettschwager

U14'S RUGBY MATCH

Shouts from the crowd, coaches running the lines bellowing hoarsely,
Excited parents, proud and bright.
The coloured jerseys flash and bob,
In the Sunday morning light.
Our boys were pushing forward, pushing hard,
Close to the line a scrum . . . pushing, jostling, shouting
The battle in full thrust.
Limbs intertwined, bodies taught, the shrilling whistle of the ref.
The heap of bodies soften, loosen and disperse, leaving one,
One left in the mud, quiet and still - someone's child.
The noise becomes a deafening silence,
All movement slows,
Breath caught in the throat, heart stopping - then hammering, No.
The child lies still, in the cold mud amidst the electric silent huddle.
'Don't move' voices whispered 'Don't move.'
'Call 999 someone, someone please.'
A dead numbness envelops my mind, as cold and cloying
As the mud he lies in.
Incapable of speech or movement,
I have no thoughts to speak or anywhere to go.
Eyes deadened looking out, not believing.
Cold light and mud surround the child resplendent in the blue.
No, please God no . . .
My disembodied voice tries to break the silence, to no avail,
How could this happen?
What went wrong?
My heart lies on the ground, fractured and numb,
This can't be happening,
Not to my son.

Terry Connor

THE LITTLE MADONNA OF 'EL TORO'

It's Tuesday again and there she is
Infant son on knee.
Veiled in smoke, her hair's a cloud,
Her eyes as blue as the sea.

The little Madonna of 'El Toro'
Appears to have fallen from grace,
Rumour has it on the silent drum
She's got a man at her place.

The boy-child laughs,
She is vaguely aware
Of his sea-blue eyes
And soft pale hair.

No Gabriel announced his coming,
It came as rather a shock.
Seemed like one day
She was wearing her gymslip,
The next a maternity smock.

Serene, she sips her Diet Coke,
A modern icon amid the smoke.

Sheenagh MacDonald

SOMEWHERE AT THE CENTRE

Our love of words.
Shared anger and pain.
Touched somewhere at the centre
of this.

I heard your language
so fluent, expressive.
Understanding our need
to communicate
somewhere in the middle of this.

Dialogue, back and forth.
Flowing smooth through barriers
no longer there.
Our souls touched, then parted
somewhere deep inside.

We both saw something
that could have been
had life not worn us down
and left us too damaged
to hold on.

Now back to our own
journeys. Having
touched and felt a need
that could have been fulfilled.

Time now, to move on.
To find peace.

Sarah Miller

MILLENNIAL MOTHER'S DAY

At the breast of men
Gerontocracy was nourished,
Through religion, medicine and politics
Patriarchy has flourished.
So consider for a moment,
Power, sex and gender,
On this matriarchal Sabbath
Let us remember -
Asylum stays and bed-rest cures,
Tales of witchcraft and folklore's.
Spinster sisters, lesbian queens,
Think for a moment what this means,
Of each new benefit
Down the female line,
And the rights we've gained
Through the passage of time.
It has taken many deaths
To change these laws,
Most of which were not fighting
For any feminist cause.
From medical reform to legislation on stalkers,
Public toilets designed big enough for baby walkers.

Babes of autocratic Blair,
Although in number have their share,
Don't seem to get the top positions,
They're mainly backbench politicians.
In and out of Tony's favour,
Toeing party line by pager.
When a politician without a pecker
Becomes Chancellor of the Exchequer,
I will celebrate deliriously,
Because it will mean at last
We're being taken seriously.

The future is gynocracy,
To become the new democracy,
Bring down the male hypocrisy.
And if you think that's too strong,
You're wrong!
Those dicks have run the show too long.
People always telling me
Sexism no longer exists.
But how can that be true,
In a world where women
Actually want plastic tits,
And puffed up lips, nips and tucks
After dinner up-chucks.

Oh, take me to the Promised Land,
Where sanitary towels are free,
And men replace the toilet seat
When they've had a pee.
Feminism may be out of fashion,
Though it should be every woman's passion.
So daughters, sisters, friends and lovers,
Join in alliance with all mothers,
To educate the female mind
To walk the talk for womankind.

Dawn Gillespie

UNTAMED HEARTS

Untamed hearts
Run wild and free
Burning the flames of passion
Showing the beats of desire
Flowing the blood of love

Love thick and ongoing

Untamed hearts
Fiercely bite
But softly hold tight
To loved ones they grip
Whilst their wildness may rip

Untamed hearts
Cause happiness and pain
Untamed hearts
Are never the same

Their fiery passion scalds
Their secret desires scar
And their boiling blood of truth
Shows
The real love
That cannot be reached
That cannot be touched
An Untamed Heart cannot be loved.

Katy Morley

PERSEPHONE'S BREATH

The deepest blue of nights and dreams
such vivid hues across these scapes
I am standing at the crossroads
Hecate at my left
whilst about me petals swirl in a breeze
stirred by Persephone's breath

The narcotic blue of the lotus twists in my hands
I am waiting at my crossroads
now to journey
but which land?
The flower finds its seducement plain
my lips apart to receive my story
so now we see my first bloom disappear
you see my eyes
without any fear
for these darkest blues have seen true life
down deep with its mate death
in the shadows I have lurked
where mouths press cold against each other
the hunger denied
sister with brother
The sickness is mine
I take the despair
I sing with the pain
now up out of there
you see me

I am a woman.

Linda Cleary

COLOURS OF RAGE

My heart has melted from the core,
In the heat of your anger, so intense.
Flashes of hatred,
More than vivid
Green! Red! Black!
In your face.

Scarlet rage!
Scatty,
Shaking with fear and despair,
I shall not run,
For a glint of envy.

With your devil's glare
Penetrating and turning to stone,
Anyone loving the man within.

Such passion suppressed,
With pain and mistrust.
I need to face up to all of this hurt,
To help my life for the future,
And to consider all of the changes approaching.

Change comes to all of us,
Throughout our lives.
Ready or not!

Now all of the mist has risen,
Now a new day has begun,
Calmer, but shamed,
Cool, yet in focus,
No fear passes through me,
Since I've accepted change.

My home is my castle,
And here I will stay!
Secured by my kin,
Taking each day as it comes,
Feeling the wheel ever turning,
In my cycle of life,
Which has guided me here.

Ally Joyner

THE FIGURE IN THE CARPET

I will take you, said the Earth Master
Just look down at the cards
And once you can see
We will begin to fly, my child
This is the card of the Shadow
Who wanders lost in the dark
See how it fears my music
And the road into nowhere?
I will tell you why, my child
For here stands the smiling Statue
A guardian of the fallen souls
And here is the Hidden Palace
Whose violet towers are crumbling
Are you learning? Said the Earth Master
Just reach out with your mind
And when it is time
The universe will be ours, my child
This is the Lake of Drowning
Under which the Voices live
Do you hear their sad sweet singing
Like the ecstasy of angels?
I will tell you why, my child
For they have unmasked the mysteries
Of the card of the Red Riddle
And they know the secrets
Of the Burnt and Twisted Hand
You must not fear, said the Earth Master
Even when I fade away
For if you succeed
Nothing can eclipse us, my child
This is the card of the Unicorn
A symbol of lost inhibitions
And this is my Self, pointing downward
Laughing over another victim . . .

Who is this on the Twilight card?
Who is the figure writhing in chains?
Do not leave me! Help me understand why
When I stand back, its head turns away
But when I step into the picture itself
The figure and I meet face to face?

Stephanie Reise

3 DAYS AND SPACED OUT

Only three days to go
And the house will be mine
Room for me on the free settee
The comfy chair,
                    spare
No nauseating aftershave will hang in the air
on the landing
    where so often
I would have to squeeze or plead
To pass him, standing there
In front of the mirror
Or stand for hours in a lonely queue
waiting
'I need the bathroom too'
I'd call through the door
But my words would fall on deaf ears
As always they did
And now finally after years, and years
Of torment, torture, anger and tears
I will no longer have to fear that
Just as I slip to sleep
The serenity of my room will be
Smashed
His entrance announced with a
Crash of the door
   And why does he disturb me?
For nothing more
Than to tell me some trivial fact
That I won't even recall
In the morning, yawning

But soon he (in only three days)
Will go off to Uni
All packed and ready
'Now steady' I call
As the pans are added to the rapidly growing pile
Him, cooking?
Funny thought
His toast is runny
He couldn't fry up for love (maybe money?)
    But no matter to me
His space will be mine in just
Three days from now
Space
Double what I've got
A heck of a lot
In fact, tonnes of empty . . . silent . . . space
        No more of his jokes around the kitchen table
His place won't be needed
With all this fresh space
I won't be able to look up from my meal
To his grinning face
As he asks us again to join in
The new game he's just made
So often we've played them for hours on end

    Perhaps I don't want him to leave at all
Not go away but stay
I hope he will choose
To come home again soon
After all how much space
        Can one brother use?

Jess Blackett

THE LOST LOVE

What is there more beautiful than love?
What is there more pure and naively true?
Is there on this earth or in the sky above,
Another such created image as you?

To what shall I liken this feeling divine?
The sparkling dew on the morning grass,
Does not compare with this passion of mine,
Nor even fair Helen with your reflection glass.

No not Trojan Helen whose face launched the ships,
Had such tranquil youth, yet vitality clear,
Nor Cleopatra of Egypt such warm ruby lips,
Never before was there anyone so dear.

And now that you've gone without me,
I am set apart all on my own,
Incomplete like a branch awaiting the tree,
So utterly useless and helplessly alone.

Marjorie R Simpson

ESSENCE OF WOMANHOOD

Essence of womanhood, how to define.
Sensual and feminine, simply divine
Partner to man with so much love to share
Giving, not taking, and always aware.

Observing the needs of the ones she holds dear
Smiling through happiness, wiping the tear
Strong and determined yet tender and kind
Prepared for life's fast lane with others in mind.

She's somebody's daughter of whom praise is sung
A natural provider of womb for her young
Nurturer, helper, an ear to bend,
Homemaker, mother, companion and friend.

Shirley M Watson & Carolyn J Watson

A Kiss In The Dark

I remember the first time,
Felt inclined to touch your lips like cashmere
The same that caressed shoulders of sculptured stone.

Theatre drove us together
                    don't you think
Or did the dark play tricks on my mind?

You were not overly kind.
                    Distant.

Eyes did not welcome strangers
                    who pursued the heart.
They fought off temptation with
                    a cursing grin.

I stumbled between your thighs at dawn.
You pitied me.

Stroking my head like Mother.

Now run along and find another girl
                    to kiss in the dark.

J Adams

Random 'Excess' Memory

A cortex partially functioning.
Neurones ready to be fired.
Grey cells like silicon chips
gathering dust
await a systems upgrade.
We run on minimum power
not facilitating our hard drive.
Slow and inefficient programmes.
A fraction of our full operational capacity.

What abilities lie dormant
in the unused stores
of our central processing units?
If we maximise the potential of our motherboard
human networking may be possible.
We could surf our cerebral depths
to interface on the universe wide web.
If we change the way we use our software
and get connected to our brains.

Access our extended memory.
Log on to the probability
that we are now set up
to really get up and running.
Mere infants on the evolutionary scale.
Not the accomplished adults we assume we are
but, like children, ready for a steep learning curve
just beginning to fully compute.

Gale Knight

AN IDLE FANCY

No heavy sound of hobnailed boots
Only the gentle rhythm of tunics swishing
And feet marching
And the humming and the chanting
To a drum beating in Stane Street Sussex

An idle fancy as I saunter from the station,
Laden with London shopping
Along the country road stopping - looking
At ducks raking muck
In the green sedge stream

Alone in Railway Cottage, Pottersfield,
In the depths of Sussex
I ponder about time and space
Where legionaries encamped

And where I discovered something special
Pottery pieces appear as I plant Acanthus,
Reminder of Corinthian columns
That I saw once in Verona

Am I prey to flights of fancy
Or is it a figment of reality
Being aware of soldiers from Rome
Marching and chanting to a drum beating
In Stane Street

M Mattey

FREEDOM AT LAST

I look back, now that I'm happy, to my years of Hell with you
To all the mental cruelty and the beatings black and blue
I think of how I hated you for the way you put me down
Of how you scoffed and laughed at me before everyone in town
Of how you'd say 'Is she boring you?' - 'You don't have to be polite'
To anyone who'd speak to me in the pub on a Friday night
You'd swan in through the double doors with such dignity and grace
With me six steps behind you - Oh! Yes - I knew my place!
Then you'd let the handles go and look around with pride
As the doors would slam in front of me before I could step inside
I'd pretend it didn't bother me - I'd let you have your fun
Because I knew I'd get the chance one day to pack my bags and run
You wouldn't work - you wouldn't want - you won't like me to
                                                    mention
How drunk you got on a Saturday night - on the proceeds of my pension
But now that I'm free and happy - if I think of you at all
It'll be with scorn and pity - you pathetic little soul

Aileen Anderson

OUT OF THE DARKNESS

Whatever I told them
whatever I said
they never would listen
they never believed
they only would see him and hear what he said
'cause he was the father, he was the King
and I was a child

He always was righteous
I always was wrong
whenever he raped me
however I cried
he never would listen
'cause he was the justice, he was the law
and I was his child

And now that he's gone
he's left me a wasteland
with little to grow
but still
I am hopeful
'cause I am the Queen now
and he is just dead

Ann Roselyn

WHERE WERE YOU?

Mother, where were you?
I cried for you in vain.
I called out in my sleep
And during the day again.
What was happening to my body?
Why do I have this pain?
Mother, where are you?
I cried again, and again.

Mother, where were you?
The day I married in white.
I looked around everywhere,
But you were not in sight.
What was going to happen
In the darkness of the night?
Mother, where are you?
Tell me what is right.

Mother, where were you?
The day my child was born
I knew not what to do,
In those hours before the dawn.
But when I held him in my arms,
I knew I was not like you,
My child will never cry out,
Mother, where were you?

H Trent

KNOWING

Snatched words from
the confines of the toilet
enhance my real status.
Conversations never completed,
for time is never on our side.
Tears are shed for a wanting beyond belief.
My name will never be used within your circle,
My face will never smile on your familiar ground,
only there will hatred be my friend.
Despair walks hand in hand
with patience, in our life.
Longing jumps on the back of love
to carry us on
to the next hurried exchange.

Nettie Bennett

UNTITLED
(In memory of my late husband who died in 1993, aged only 47)

Remembering;
sunny days
loving ways
long walks
gentle talks
dreaming
scheming
tears
fears
sad eyes
goodbyes
separate ways
cloudy days
loving ever
forgetting - never

Christine Jones

TODAY WOMAN

Today I am a woman, mother, wife
Too busy with everyday comings, goings, life
Too fast to stop and notice the trees
Their big trunks, green leaves stirring in the breeze.

I want my child to see them then
How I saw them when I was ten.
These trees they were our surrounds and life
In the playground no care, dreams, hopes, no strife.

Time, it's hard to catch, running along technology advanced,
Can I keep up? - I have to for it's my child's life
The future ours, dreams, hopes, the challenge, the strife
Yes I am woman, mother, wife, Leader-woman in this life.

Maria Masood

MURDER

A ceiling, a floor,
Four walls, locked door.
One small barred window, lets in no light,
Midnight air impairs your sight.
Cold steel metal, bars your escape,
Darkness that fails, distorts every shape.
Cramped the room, that fails your dream,
Of mountains, ocean, bubbling stream.
For in the corner, stale and old,
Bread and water of scum and mould.
Tomorrow the same, the next and so on,
Mustn't be touched its smell is too wrong.
The lock is turned, you march to a wall,
A command is ordered a shot, you fall.
'About turn' and away, you're left alone,
Grasses and flowers, one tall grey stone.
The flowers mark your grave, the stone tells your life,
You fought for your country and died for your wife.

Claire D Dennis

FROM THE CRADLE TO THE GRAVE

Today's child is the voice of tomorrow
A vision of the future, listen to his sorrow
Listen to the misery, poverty, he portrays
For he is the child who had the misfortune of being born today

I'm the one whose childhood was a disgrace
Rejected by the so-called human race
I am the child born out of sin
I'm the whimpering sound discovered in a bin
I'm the unwanted soul whose cry
Echoes through the night
I am the one they hide out of sight
I'm the child forced to beg off the street
Never knew my dad, neglected by my mum, no food to eat
I am the child who suffers sexual abuse
Repeatedly, silently seduced
I've never known love, never felt safe and sound
I would do anything to be cuddled, to be Mummy's little angel
Instead of beaten and kicked to the ground
I dream of life filled with happiness
School day frolics, new clothes, lots of friends
But I'm the one who's poverty stricken
Yesterday's clothes and pitied by friends who pretend
I'm the child pushed into adolescence before my time
Introduced to drugs, alcohol and crime
Thinking only of my next fix
Hallucinating, the mind playing tricks
As night closes in, icy winds
Send shivers down my spine
While the world sleeps safe and sound. I
Lay awake alone, a cardboard box for my home
And my roof is the wide open sky
I've never known love, never felt safe and sound
For I am the child with no background
I'm the one who learnt to be streetwise
Where evil works, shadows lurk

I'm the child in disguise
I'm the child who sadly mistook love for lust
Became a punch bag to someone I thought I could trust
I'm the child whose infant was taken into care
Unable to cope, with promises of hope, for a child
Whose life would be a nightmare
I am the child who's old before my time
Tired of life's heartaches, had my fill of life's slime
I've never known love, never felt safe and sound
From the cradle to the grave, I've been everyone's slave
But now I'm homeward bound
My journey's end. No more will I pretend
With God, I know I'm safe and sound
I was that child lost, but now found.

Sonia Coneye

MERMAID'S PURSE

Egg case of dogfish
Found halfway up a dune.
Praa Sands.
May.
Blown by wind,
Carried by tide,
From the sea's depths?
Found.
Empty.
But four 'claws' protruding
From each corner.
Hard, seemingly brittle
(Yet pliable too).
Egg case.
Curious.
There, for the finding.

Jinty Knowling Lentier

A Successful Woman

As a child, life's lessons:
'Beauty is only skin deep'
Beauty fades.
Charisma, honesty, intelligence
are obviously more important to life
than sex.

The philosophical articles I have read,
the interesting people I have met
and am still to meet
do not figure for society's women.
What they need is to dye their hair
and diet when they reach forty.
Then they will feel fulfilled.
As I read in a magazine
the other day.

What's my role in life?
Well, it was to be natural,
with a depth of character,
well read.
Now? Now if I were to have children
what would I advise them?

Fiona Burns

NIGHT VIEWING

Flicking through the channels,
Know that she will wait,
Till the mood arises,
If it's not too late.
Test the body temperature
If it feels all right,
Fill at least one cavity,
In her otherwise empty life.
Bonded to an alien ,
On a piece of paper,
Cast aside forsaken bride,
Like discarded litter,
Once there was a magic,
Or so there seemed to be,
Was this life or dreaming?
The romantic in me?
I look on as you're sleeping,
In our double bed,
Single life, once man and wife,
Togetherness is dead.

Brenda O'Hagan

ANSWERS CAME THERE NONE

Is there order amongst the chaos?
Are there any answers to be had?
Why all the fighting and all the wars?
Why does all the news sound so bad?
Why the death and destruction?
Why the hunger and the need?
Why is everything so unbalanced?
Why so much evil in our seed?
Why do we wreck God's creation?
With pollution and acid rain?
Why cause new killer diseases?
Why endanger life to gain?
No - there isn't really an answer,
Now that destruction has gone so far.
We have to face this tragedy,
And cope with things as they are.
We cannot turn the clock backwards,
To the future we must aim.
We can never solve all the problems,
But we can seriously play life's game.
We must continually search for peace,
We must try to see the world fed.
We must try to halt the destruction,
Before all our resources are dead.
For into this world come the young ones,
They must take all these problems on,
Will they shake their heads in bewilderment,
And wonder, like me, what went wrong?

C Harris

THE TIDE

The tide is drifting away now,
It's drawing back into the distance; with it goes the shawl of
                                    darkness and madness,
The legacy of my youth, the blackness and death of my past.
It's receding now, watch it go, it moves slowly away from me,
Going further and further into the distance.
It's drawing back now, can't you see it go, watch it move away
                                        from me now,
Slower and slower, but it's going from me.

Look at me now, it's leaving me well alone,
It will never come back,
It is a tide that will go further and further away from me.

Look at me now, see me now, how I stand
I am clear and I shine forth.
I radiate in the bright light of the moon,
Look at the pebbles around me at my feet,
Look how they support me
Look how they gather around me
They too are sparkling in the moonlight.
Look at their glow, look at our glow.

We glow brightly and the tide recedes further away
Into the darkness where I will never meet it again,
Where I will never see it again.

See my sparkle, see my glow.
See me radiate in the bright light of my entirety.

Caroline Delancey

THE BENEFACTOR

Why does everyone think you are so great?
Is it because they believe you relate?
As I watch you listen and take your ease
Seemingly everyone sits at your knees!

You promise them all that you 'will be there'
'Call if you need me, you know how I care!'
What would you do if we all came together?
Sat at your feet and stayed there forever?

You give out a hope, that cannot be met
There are so many people you tend to forget
But you stay in their head become part of their heart
And out of their memory you never depart.

You hold out your hand, say 'Be part of my life'
Then take us all home to your family, and wife
Orphans and widows, the ill and insane
Troop in with pleasure to view your domain.

'This is my family, this is my home'
With pride in your voice you show all that you own.
You hand out the coffee, you hand out the tea
And if they are lucky they get wine, like me!

You are showing us something that we've never had.
You are so lucky, and we should be glad!
We admire all your qualities, we think you are great
But there is no way at all to us you relate!

You raise expectations we believe to be true
That you like us so much we've become close to you.
But all that you do at the end of the day
Is show what we can't have, and send us away.

So here's to the benefactor who held out the chalice
And produced within each of us, envy and malice.

Helen H Hayman

A PHOTOGRAPH

A piece of paper large or small
A vision printed to recall
A precious moment, a treasured place
A new experience, a parted face.
Some were happy, some were sad,
but all were lived through, good and bad,
new or old, perhaps battered and thin
all were taken, in this world we live in
healthy or crippled, sighted or blind,
Our fondest memories are brought to mind.

Christine Joiner

FULFILMENT

You've got a nice house,
what more do you want? He
questioned,

exasperated

by my
being me
and
not being
as he thinks
I should
be . . .

cosseted in Anaglypta.

Jenny Hope

MY BABY

Just a baby in my arms
Need to keep her free from harm
Little button nose and eyes
An angel from heaven in disguise
The love I felt, on her bestowed
Loved her lots and helped her grow
Watched her changing day by day
Taught her lots in work and play
Changed from babe to toddler
Everyone so proud of her
Left behind her childhood toys
Turned attention then to boys
Then to teenage years she grew
Gave her wisdom that I knew
Whether I was right or wrong
Wanted her to grow up strong
Made mistakes within my life
Caused me woe and even strife
When happiness had passed me by
Felt that I could sit and cry
Always did what I thought best
Sometimes wrong like all the rest
Before the path that she must take
To womanhood, just for her sake
There is something she should know
How much I really love her so.

Gina Sturt

CHOICES

A woman is a wearer of many different hats,
In the year 2000 it is a well known fact,
We have so many choices now, we don't know where to start,
Should I work or stay at home or juggle each and every part?
Colleague, wife and mother, teacher, nurse and many more,
We try our best at all these roles in the hope we'll know the score.
To somehow fill our lives with the things we enjoy the best,
It is not always easy to fit in a well earned rest!
'Quality time' is crucial we hear the experts say,
So stress relief and massage we're supposed to have each day.
I have yet to find a woman, who has time for all of these,
She's much too busy trying, each and everyone to please.
Let us all as women realise, of *'us'* we need to think,
To keep our heads above the water and our sanity not to sink,
In the end I hope, that we will all have learned,
We cannot all be everything to everyone in turn!

Andrea Barker

WHAT IS A MOTHER?

A mother is someone who is always there,
To help you with problems and show that she cares.
She's there to help with all aspects of life,
From being a mother to being a wife!

What can I say about this mother of mine,
She's the best friend that I'll ever find.
Nobody else could ever take her place,
Or replace the great smile that's on her face!

She has always been there for me,
Whatever my problem may be.
Life hasn't always dealt her a very good card,
But she's managed no matter how hard!

When I have asked, 'how she has coped?'
Her answer has been that her faith gives her hope.
The advice she has given has always been good,
But I didn't always take it like I should!

My mother is very gentle and kind,
And always has everyone else on her mind.
Mother I have a wish that I hope will come true,
And it is that I will grow to be like you!

Mum you are to me,
The very best, that you can be.
My hope is now that you do know,
How very much I love you so!

Jackie Illsley

RAINDROPS

The torrent of hormones
We must bear
The onslaught of puberty
Spots and pubic hair

Pre-menstrual syndrome
Cravings and needs
Cuddles and chocolate
And understanding please!

Swirls of creativity
Ebb and flow, amongst
The emotional highs and lows.

Ovulation, copulation . . . pregnancy!
A woman's amazing
Gift to conceive.

Labour is hard, but necessity
A journey from womb
To reality!

Overwhelming feeling of love and pride
Blanket you from the world outside
Your special moment
Forever in time.

And what of the menopause
That which we fear
The shedding of fertility
May raise a tear.

You've finished the rollercoaster
Of hormonal swings
You have balanced stability
Enjoy what it brings.

Kate Rees

HER DAY

As she walked along the shoreline
And she watched the storm at sea,
The waves washed out her footprints
Any trace of where she'd been.

She realised as the lightning flashed
All the anger raging there,
She knew once more this storm would pass
And she wished she didn't care.

But so many times he's hurt her
Too many times she's cried,
Too many times she's sat alone
When he should be by her side.

This time it was different
As the storm within her grew,
This time she felt stronger
This time she felt she knew.

As the lightening flashed, she realised
As her footsteps left their mark,
She was tired of being swept away
No more broken heart.

As the lightening flashed, the storm had died
She'd left her mark at last,
She'd washed away the storm clouds,
She'd put him in her past.

With the lightening flash, her strength was born
She knew she could move on,
One lightning flash had proved to her
She didn't need this storm.

As she closed this chapter in her life
And the storm clouds rolled away,
She saw one lightning flash
And she knew this was her day.

Pam Law

REVENGE

You'll never know how much I miss
The sweetness of your lips,
You'll never know how much I miss
The touch of your finger tips,
You'll never know the pain I feel
Deep inside my heart,
You'll never know the pain I feel
Since we have been apart,
I hope to God you never know
The emptiness inside,
I hope to God you never know
What a lonely soul I hide,
But if you ever come to know
The emotions deep within,
If you ever come to know
The ache in every limb,
Just remember what you did to me
For this is pay back time
Just remember what you did to me
Revenge is sweet, revenge is mine.

Tam

CHRISTMAS NIGHT

Nobody knows the way I feel tonight
Everything's wrong and nothing is right
Nothing to do, nowhere to go
Oh how much I miss you so
It's Christmas time once again
I try to make it just the same
As when you were once here
But it really brings it home to me
How very much alone are we
Maybe it's this time of year
When everyone is full of cheer
That I feel this way
I try my best to get the things
The presents that Santa Claus brings
To see the look upon their faces
It really puts you through the paces
But things could never be the same
Even though you admit to the blame
It does not take away the pain
I feel tonight
For two wrongs don't make a right
And once again it's Christmas night
And we are all alone.

Elizabeth Leach

THE GIRL THAT ONCE WAS

The baby cries, the husband stares, and the mother's drained of hope.
She's in need of love, the love she gave away,
To a fragile child and a man who lost his pay.

Tired of waiting, dreams are gone,
Nobody can relate to the girl that once was.

She sings a lullaby to her empty soul as she cradles the baby's food.

As the hand hits her face and the tears run dry, she prays to a God,
Desperately hugging herself tight, wishing to be held.
The harsh voice whispers again and again, sharp as a knife
As it stabs itself in, into her tranquil soul.

'You're only a shadow poised on a mantelpiece,
Like generations of women before.
The men will always reflect the light.'

She rocks the baby between her mind
And touches its skin, the foundation of the future.

The woman chooses her path, but as before, it's not for herself,
It's for the fragile child.

Lucy Norris

AFTER

In my twenties the wall came down
His name is David
He removed the bricks
One by one by one by one
Don't think he expected to have such fun
After it all came down
Lots of ice water
Lots of boulders
Lots of me he did not know
To him . . . well, it was a blow
He recovered fast and helped me clear
Worked through the lot
Including my fear
Lots of me I did not know
For me . . . well, the greatest blow
It's all done now
My path is cleared
The damage reversed
Including my fear
Nothing scares me
I have gone higher
No more the ice
I am now fire.

Marsha Durok

LIFE AFTER JOHN

Time to be tidy now I'm alone,
Now that our children have grown up and flown.
Time to be tidy, things in their place,
No need for hurry, scurry or race.
I look at the clock, it's only just ten.
I've washed up and tidied and dusted again.

Jessica Jarlett

KISS THE DRAGON

I kissed the dragon's fiery breath
And visualised the devil
I thought of David Bowie reaching Ziggy Stardust level
Though not intoxicated
Nor taking any pills
I felt I'd sipped a potion
As I sifted through the bills
I've read some Harry Potter books
Of wizards not of witches
And watched some period dramas
Of ladies and their riches
But when I'm in my office
I hear the people ask
'Does her face become enshrouded,
with a little coloured mask?'
'She opens up those letters with a
Blade sharp and serrated,
But her mind's not on the job,
She always seems so agitated.'
Yes, I kissed the fiery dragon
Sorry did I mean his breath
At work my strange imagination
Leads the dragon to his death.

Tracy Gwynne

GIVING BIRTH IS EASY

My sister was having a baby
Who was happier, her or me?
I have one who's nearly five
And one who's almost three.

My sister was having a baby
We talked of this and that.
Of how easy it was to give birth
And how hard it was ridding the fat.

My sister was having her baby
The waters had broken just fine.
There's nothing to having a baby
It's easy, it just takes time.

My sister was having her baby
My two were like shelling peas.
My sister has taken three days now
My two had popped out with ease.

I'm frightened now for my sister
She's pushing but there's just nothing there.
She's pale as she lies on the bed now
It's easy. No, this is unfair!

The midwife is suddenly worried
The doctor is called for at last!
She has to have an emergency section
'Will it hurt?' she asks.

My sister has had her baby.
He arrived, now he's warm and fed.
She mutters, 'It's not bloody easy!'
'I lied but I'm so proud of you!' I said.

R J Davies

THE LABOURS OF LOVE

Selfless shopping,
cooking meals.
Daily drudgery of dishes
and scraping pots.
Pointless repetition
of boring housework.
Cleaning clothes
and sewing buttons.
Bearing babies
and rearing same.
Laughing at jaded jokes
and post-booze braggadocio.
Family ego-boosting,
totally unrequited.
Unwaged, unappreciated.
A life-time sentence
of hard labour.
   the continuing acceptance
       of which,
  only
   Love
   can explain.

Marjorie V Quigley

ONCE . . .

Once, we walked
through glistening grass
with jewelled blades.
The sunlight sharp, vivid.
Eyes squinting and faces aglow.
Snuffly noses and steamy breath.
A leafy carpet of
red, brown, orange.
Velvet, golden mornings.

Now . . . we ride
through shining whiteness
a threadbare cloak.
Reality is hazy, opaque.
Vision dulled and lips blued.
Blanched faces and chattering teeth.
A marble flooring of
grey, white, silver.
Crystal, alabaster days.

Once . . . we walked.
Now . . . we ride.

Denise Wells

WOMAN

The woman sits in darkness
Rocking gently in her chair.
Like lightning through the thunder
Is her sun-kissed, golden hair.
Staring at her sewing
With blue, rain-sparkled eyes.
Crying for the happy times,
Weeping at the lies.
Guiding the needle
Through the worn, family quilt,
Stitching the holes
Through which her love had spilt.
Wrapped in a rainbow
Cowering from the hand
That left her dreams crashing
Like a castle made of sand.
She knows she has the power
And is willing to be free
But she wants to be requited
For the love he could not see.
Reaching out for beauty
Whilst covering her scars,
Peering out at freedom
Through her prison window bars.
Longing to escape him,
Wondering if she can
For she is servant to the master
Mistress to the man.

Rhiannon Cousins

WOMEN'S PROGRESS

Dear Mrs Pankhurst,

              How I wish you could be here to see
How much women accomplished in the twentieth century.
You started, we continued, but you opened up our eyes -
Taught us to fight for fairness - make them listen to our cries.

In 1939 when men were called up into war,
The women had to do the work which men had done before.
Land girls toiled hard in farmers' fields with great agility
And high-positioned women proved their true ability.

We have good educations and we strive like any man,
With equal salaries which is (supposedly) the plan,
Yet many times we struggle just to prove our equal right
For still existing chauvinists create the need to fight.

We've earned our independence and have striven with such pains
To prove our worth commercially, employing women's brains.
No longer are we household slaves for young men do their share,
We don't have lots of children with no time or cash to spare.
Gone are the days we cleaned and scrubbed and cooked the whole day through,
We're citizens of value, in our own right, thanks to you.

In government positions now, we see female MPs
Who diligently toil to sort the wood from all the trees.
The year of 1979 was revolutionary -
A woman held the highest post offered in this country!

As Prime Minister, Mrs Thatcher showed how she was strong,
Standing against the unions proving predecessors wrong.
She helped our cause for jealous men looked up in admiration
Of how she carried out office with credit to our nation.

Well, Mrs Pankhurst, there's no doubt we've come a long, long way,
But you're the reason we do all the things we do today.
You showed determination, courage, suffered for the cause -
We women of this century remain,

Thankfully yours,

Joy Saunders

THE SEPARATED SWAN

I'm too young
to be a hag
pinched and severe
but this is how I feel -
this spring
there's been no mercy

I cannot bear
the blossomed trees, the hum,
the resurrection
of the bees -
this new-born light
that tugs at me

Half-healed
the wounded swan
returns to seek her mate
The enchantment's gone -
new feathers
guard her scars

and she's come *so far*
And with a rush of wings
she seeks to land
but finds the oldest lake
has frozen
deep within me

But I'm *too young*
to be a hag!
Goddess!
you let your temples fail,
your maidens
beat their veils against the rock

What is this
'Out damned spot!'
you've bred in us!

Is it yet too late?
Shall I sit and wait
beside the wrought-iron gate
my potions doomed
to crumble unto dust
unless the stranger comes

For this swan's mute
she cannot even call
his name
                through all her tears,
                        through all the years
                                she sought for him . . .

Nora Leonard

BEYOND THE GARDEN

Fairy whispers on the breeze
-And who but you could know of these?
Fairy thoughts and fairy pleasures
Far beyond all human measures
Dancing as all fairies do
Happy mischief making too
Twirling round all petal clad . . .
Under fleeting clouds and moon
Softly move to fairy tune

Fairy whispers on the wind
Silver web around them spinned
And only you could know such things
Soft sighing sounds and beating wings
Childhood dreams naive and bright
Tender thoughts that still the night
Feather light and fancy free
Fairy people - those are we
Look far beyond the sun and see.

Marilyn Hodgson

THE BEGINNING

Light flutterings awaken me, the feel of butterfly wings
Small movements from within me as a brand new life begins.
Protectively I rest my hand upon my abdomen
And sit and marvel at this gift - a daughter or a son.
A child made through tenderness unique in every way
The ultimate bond from him to me to cherish every day.

Karen D James

LOVERS NO MORE

Your lips touch mine, gently as a butterfly.
My heart races, feelings running high.
Bodies fusing one last time.
The hardness of yours, the softness of mine.
'Til, when morning comes, you say goodbye.
Tears prick my eyes and I start to cry.
Why do we love when it hurts so much?
Why do we yearn for another's touch?
No answer to this, but at its height.
Love is like a blinding light.
When gone it leaves a darkened void.
Gone the shared pleasures we once enjoyed.
Yet eventually we forget the pain
When that blinding light strikes again.

P Hopkins

THE BARMAID

Have respect,
Do not reject,
The girl who works so hard at life,
You don't understand,
With your pint in your hand.
Stand and mock,
You drunken lot,
And pretend to be something you're not.
Because in the day,
Likely than not.
You do a worse job,
Than the one I've got!

Christine McGrath

NEW WOMEN

New women's estate can only compare with
a young fledglings attempt to take to the air.

The struggle to resist dependence on others
to reach out and grapple with own life decisions.

Family, career and life inspirations, choices which
now belong to her generation.

Husband, children, home, career,
all shape her future over the years.

A juggling act she needs to perform,
to satisfy self as well as her spawned.

Finally there she hopes contentment is hers
and vows she's a lot better off than her predecessors.

Those women who sacrificed freedom to give her the vote.
She will not give in to those who provoke.

And at last she takes to the air, she tries out her wings,
but she need not despair.

She believes in herself, not what others may think.
Life's far too important when one's on the brink.

Margaret Goodfellow

THE WORST WITCH

I collected twigs
wading through
mud
searching for
the best

Only the best is good enough for
my daughter

Later
your smile as you rode
on your broomstick
made it
worthwhile

The worst witch
but the best
daughter.

Alison Southern

PURGE PUKE PUTREFY

Oh God. Obliterate me,
I'm carried away with the ecstasy of abasement.
Oh God. Mortify my flesh.

I'm constantly praying for emptiness
So that I should be worthy to be fuelled by bread.
The problem is getting it down without choking on it.

Temptation comes next.
For me all tempter is eating.
For me all temptation is to dispose of.

Oh God. How can I keep on existing.
Oh God. I can no longer talk at you.
I want my madness to ease as a philosopher's peace.

Oh God. I have only prayed to know the worst,
and wish as if my head would tell no seemingly doubtful tale.
To live. To die. Whatever . . .

. . . God. That bread is mine.

Tarryn L Workman

MY DESTINY

I blunder, senseless, through this life,
Blind to beauty, deaf to sound
Of music, merry-making, laughter
And all the wonders all around.

A baby, child, an adolescent
Now a woman, just another,
So many like me, fearing future,
Of being a wife, of being a mother.

What lies behind me I can't change,
What lies in front I cannot alter,
I travel forwards, lost and lonely,
Every step I fear and falter.

So who am I? Where do I go
From here? I am afraid to try
To alter destiny, time marches
On, and will, until I die.

Sarah Cheetham

PARTNERS

I do not stand alone.
With you I have found acceptance.
Believe love, hope, strength.
Words without speech,
Caresses through the air.
Kisses without lips,
Happy teardrops.

You do not stand alone.
With you I am, whatever.
Sea teardrops,
Angry words not meaning,
Hearts don't tear,
My believe love hope strength you have,
Completely,
Infinitely.

We stand together,
We must remember,
On our side,
Laughter,
Disappointments,
We share,
Believe love hope strength, courage.
To
Trust
To
Be.

Rosa

A Mother, Like All The Others

With determination, I pull myself onto my right side.
With resignation, I sit up, slide sideways and off the bed.
It's time for action.

With cheerfulness, I enter the bedrooms and awake each child.
With persuasiveness, I chivvy them to get up, wash and dress.
It is breakfast time.

With care, I check each has food, homework, instruments
                                                and games kit.
With patience, I wait for the lift on my van to slowly rise.
We leave for their school.

Now I am home again, what shall it be?
For just a few hours I am wonderfully free.
Should I be firm and do cleaning or mending?
Are there letters to write or serious things pending?
Maybe I'll swim, or go down to the shop.
The piano's more fun than wielding a mop.
Perhaps I'll go visiting. If so, where to?
Until they come back, no one cares what I do.

With anticipation, I await the noisy homecoming.
With interest, I learn of the day's successes and failures.
Now they are hungry.

With readiness, I listen to the little ones read their books.
With enjoyment, I hear a variety of instruments.
It's time to relax.

With contentment, I let them snuggle up close for a story.
With love, I tuck them up, kiss them and give them big goodnight hugs.
But there's a surprise.

As I leave the room, my eldest daughter says,
'Mummy, I can't imagine what it would be like to have
                                    a mother who can walk.'

D F Pargeter

NO LONGER NEXT DOOR OUR FAMILY

When I married thirty years ago
A house could be bought for three hundred pounds
No one wanted to live in the country
They all wanted the buzz of the towns.

We weren't classed as posh as we just worked down the road
Hardly any of the young owned a car
On Saturday night we'd go out on the bus
To the pictures not very far.

Now my children are grown and the very same house
Is worth fifty thousand or so
Now no one wants to live in the town
And our children have nowhere to go.

The houses are taken by well to do folks
Who poison our air with their cars
Travelling miles to work and supermarket
And going out to meals and bars.

The newcomers can't mend a wall or a ditch
They are not friendly, helpful or nice,
I really worry 'Where will our kids live?'
Because they just cannot afford the price.

Ann Abbott

A SIMPLE LIFE

I lived by the river when I was small
And never wanted to come in at all
We played outside the whole day through
The sun always shone and the skies were blue.

When into the teens I did grow
Life had its highs as well as low
My working life did then begin
And my life took a change from within.

I married when I was twenty-two
And with lots of makeshift we had to do
Washing machines were a great delight
Of fridge freezers, there was no sight.

When the children arrived we had to be able
To always provide food for the table
This was a happy time, with lots of fun
Another phase in my life had begun.

The boys grew up and both left home
So once more we were Darby and Joan
When suddenly, life took on a new hue
A bundle arrived all dressed in blue.

Grandchildren had come on the family scene
And this is the best life has ever been
Our children and grandchildren visit a lot
We love to see them from biggest to tot.

Jill Dryden

A Woman's Thing

I'm feeling out of sorts today,
When I try to make breakfast
I knock over the tray,
I spill my tea,
I walk into the door,
I shout at my husband,
I don't know what for.
Why can't the children
Sit quiet and still?
Why do I feel it'd be easy to kill?
My head's in a spin,
I feel bloated and fat,
Now I've tripped over that damn, stupid cat.
Diagnosis is easy,
What's wrong with me?
I'm simply suffering from PMT.

Wendy Bayliss

WOMEN MOVING FORWARD?

Women's roles have advanced in many a way,
We now have Equal Opportunities . . . or so men say.
We are allowed to drive, often much better than blokes,
Yet we are still the brunt of 'women driver' jokes.
We are able to work for 7 days a week,
But if an opinion is wanted, we're not allowed to speak.
We can vote for who can be in power and run the country for us,
Yet when we complain about women's rights we are said
                                        to be making a fuss.
A woman vicar, a fire woman and many other roles at last,
But have we really moved much further on, than women of the past?

L M Patterson

24/7 MUM

The day doesn't start
And the night doesn't end
It's a twenty four hour a day job
Being a mother, so demanding
A wife, housekeeper, nanny, lover.

Feeding the baby
Eyes half shut
My toddler running around
I notice the dust on top of the TV
Ignore it for now I sigh.

Baby has a nap
Toddler watches TV
Things are calm, just for a while
Now for ironing and cleaning
No time to rest for Mum.

Housework's finished, maybe a tea?
But just as the kettle boils
Baby awakes
Toddler is bored
'Read me a book' he cries.

Toddler on one knee
Baby on the other
'Once upon a time' I start
Their little faces looking at me
Their teacher, their mother, their life.

The day doesn't start
And the night doesn't end
It's such a demanding job
But my love for my children is so complete
It makes it all worthwhile.

Paula Ray

EXPECTATIONS

You want to live with me
In the house that I furnished
You'll bring all you have
Which is nothing I need
Once there
You'll say you love me
Spend all your money
Leaving the cupboard bare
Wanting clean clothes to wear
Looking for a mammie
Who pays the bills without troubling you
Who is a clairvoyant -
All day her eye on you
The sole focus of her attention
Who you can throw tantrums at and cling to
Who is your nursemaid
Counsellor
Entertainer
Listener
Who can hold back the tide with one hand
And polish the stars with the other
Who will always take you in her arms like a child
No matter what you do
And give you sex whenever you want
Tell me something,
What do you think I want out of life?

Tracy Patrick

SHIRLEY VALENTINE 2000

To my family,
Consumed by my boredom I,
Decided to write you this,
Note to describe to you,
Just how dull my life is . . .

Day in, day out, the same old bone,
Being a mother and a wife,
(Though I don't mean to moan),
Swallowed by my housework and tedious repetition,
Of taking out the rubbish, and washing *your* dishes.

I'm no fool, so please do not titter,
(Would it be a good time to mention that I'm really not bitter),
But I am woman, hear me roar,
Though not loud enough to disturb the neighbours next door.

I demand some respect and recognition,
And some occasional, voluntary help with the dishes,
My life is being wasted on daytime TV,
Dreaming of an escape whilst watching Oprah Winfrey.

I feel like a caged bird, ready to take flight,
Though my wings are pinned down by my domestic plight.
A little assistance would not go amiss,
And some kind of social life would be bliss.

One last thing I'd just like to mention,
Just one final bone of contention,
When you read this note I won't be at home,
As I've run off with the postman, and we're moving to Rome!

Nadine Parker

UNTITLED

I have wanted to know your name since forever. Alas!
Knowing your name has not brought me closer to you.
Mistily I move towards, away from,
Towards, away from
The unchanging Truth.

I place my own hands inside my own head
And twist my mind round
To face myself.
In the Truth I would be.
But I still have not enough of that
Which makes us make the jump.

I reassured myself that with time, I would
Small step by small step, no! What I know as
Safe step by safe step, get there.

But it seems that reality is not made of that,
For if we move about in that which
We claim to know,
We wonder aimlessly in the safety of this world
And are
Thus continuously lost.

Change in our own safe illusionary world
That we create, is no change at all.

Only when we are disturbed enough
Are we forced to make a true change,
Like it
Or not.

Basia Palka

OLD GODS

Whatever became of the old gods,
the gold god and stones? Triple
goddess and sacred spring -
we worshipped and
bowed down, but
now they're all gone -
burned up, paved over and around,
unable to receive our sacrifice
and yet . . .

A few remain in museums.
God of the sea, Poseidon
aims his spear in Athenian
gallery and who, seeing his perfection,
can prevent a stir of belief?

A few survive their passionate past.
Surrounded by silk, marigolds
and mirrors, a deity can actually
be touched in Delhi.

Archaeologists dig up parcels
of child bones in mezzo-American
worship sites. We do not
want to understand the sacred
jaguar. He seems totally cruel.

We do recognise the bronze
bull on Wall Street. There are many
worshippers in the market.
But isn't it pagan to make sacrifice
while hoping for long term gain?

Oh, whatever became of the old gods,
the gold god and stones, triple
goddess, and sacred spring?
Paved over and around, torn up,
burned down, and yet . . .

Mary Helen Detmer

WIND OF CHANGE

Woman's work, well
It's never done
So the old saying
From well-worn pun.

Where's my dinner?
I need a clean shirt,
Get on with it,
Shovel the dirt.

Baby's crying,
Now there's a surprise,
Guess who's turn it is?
Take the first prize.

It's your turn darling
On your nelly,
I carried the problem for nine months,
I had the fat belly.

Ann Weavers

UNTITLED

These modern times I hear them say
But I don't see it every day.

Women now are better off than they were before
So why are some still saying, 'Oh, I walked into a door?'

Society enlightened, we're aware, we'll do our bit
But in my other ear, I hear
'You've made your bed so lie in it.'

Depression of the twenties, making every penny count,
No time back then to get 'The Blues,'
Oor wee Mary's needin' shoes,
She's being ridiculed at school
While Ma man's drunk and playing the fool.

Depression of the twenties? Doesn't happen anymore?
Allow me to invite you in and see what lies behind my door.

Gillian Ferguson

IF LOSING YOU CAN CAUSE SUCH PAIN

If losing you can cause such pain
this silent ending to our war,
I cannot bear to love again.

Better to lose (the old refrain)
than never love. I'll love no more
if losing you can cause such pain.

My public face masks the red stain
but my still bleeding wounds are sore;
I cannot bear to love again.

Better to barter flesh for gain?
Ask any bought, but heart-whole, whore.
If losing you can cause such pain.

I will cut out my heart. Refrain
from feeling. Make of life a chore.
I cannot bear to love again.

I'll wrap my heart in cellophane
enclosed behind an air-tight door.
If losing you can cause such pain
I cannot bear to love again.

Rae McIntyre

LETTERS FOR LINGUISTS

Take a letter Miss Jones, her boss he said
A French Letter in bed Miss Jones
Was what he thought instead
She looked into his languid eyes
And lust was what she read.

Perhaps you'd care to dine with me
I'll see you are well fed
Fed with seeds of plenty
Seeds I'd gladly shed
If I could take you to my bed.

She looked at him with knowing eyes
She read all he'd not said
The book was all too familiar
The sheets were all well read.

He looked and knew she'd seen inside
He could not penetrate
He withdrew and tossed her on one side
She had not taken the bait.

He knew her eyes were opened wide
As once he'd seen her legs
And in an attempt to preserve male pride
He castigated her instead.

Charmon Westwood

HOUSE FOR SALE

House for sale. But who knows the heartache behind
Those two words written there.
The house now stands empty,
But once there was plenty of laughter that rang through the air.

Young children have played on those green lawns,
That apple tree once held a swing.
But who knows what comes in the future,
Or the sorrow that passing years bring.

For children must grow independent
And one day have homes of their own.
Like a bird from the nest they must leave you
And then you find you're quite alone.

You no longer need that old nursery,
For memories are all that are there
And for sale is now hung,
On that old apple tree in place of the swing that was there.

Edna Bagshaw

SKIN GAME

When I was ten
Gran said
Consolingly
'You've got good bones.'
I wanted to be pretty.

When I was twenty
Boss said
Admiringly
'You've a good brain.'
I wanted to be beautiful.

When I was thirty
He said
Indulgently
'You're a good wife.'
I wanted to be sexy.

When I was forty
Salesgirl said
Doubtfully
'It's a little youthful.'
I wanted to be glamorous.

Now I'm . . . older
I say
Defiantly
I want to be *me*.

Caroline Eatherden

UNITE

My stomach has tingles,
My head feels so light,
For the first time we can be
Alone tonight.

As your hand greets my skin,
A rush down my spine,
Electric emotions,
Are yours and mine.

Our lips now meet,
Gently at first,
The passion increasing,
I feel I could burst.

You caress my body,
Grasp your arm round my waist,
Your hand cups my jaw,
Your wanting I taste.

I need to feel your
Strength overtake,
I now want to love you
And love we now make.

As momentum is gathered,
I feel we are one,
This moment, alone,
The barrier's gone.

Victoria Hart

PARK BENCH

'What about me'
said he
holding her hand tight -
her face turned away,
was it the sun in her eyes
or was it pain
her face lined and strained
her face turned -
he looked
at her face in pain
the face that turned from him,
he looked with his youth in vain
and remembered the love in her.
They sat close
on a park bench
in autumn.

Elizabeth Nova

MY WORST ENEMY

He's back, although he is never far away, for the last
Seven years he has ruled my life one way or another,
His name, 'Arthritis'. He stalks his prey like an angry
Lion, devouring everything in his path, he eats away at
My daughter's bones, leaving her like a shipwreck in
The aftermath of a storm. Oh he is an evil man. The
Bounds of his destruction are not only physical. There
Is a need to nurture the broken child in his wake.
She requires comfort and constant attention to lift
Her above the emotional trauma his power inflicts.
Wherever we go our enemy comes too. The needles
That prick my daughter's body check if this destructive
Man has left. Still he has not gone. He is lurking in the
Background like a time bomb waiting to explode.
As time goes by, with help from drugs, this evil man is
Losing his power. It's now time to feel really good
Watching this child run and jump. The chains that held
Him tight to us are slowly rusting. The laboratory
Lights are on late at night, making the tools to break
The chains.

Caroline Read

NATURE'S CALL

Time running out there's a clock a ticking
How much longer before regret is still born
A life within awaits, it's imagined kicking
Getting even louder and louder.

Don't need a date I want a mate
To share my bed and stroke my head
To see to it that
The babies I want are fed.
To always be there day after day
Not like some who run away
If I don't answer the cry of my hormone
I could end up living alone.

That dam clock's ticking faster and faster
Time running out
If it does not happen soon my life won't count
Need to hunt my quarry down,
Don't care if their hair is black, blonde or brown,
I must pursue till he goes to ground.

Where will I find this man, this mate?
Make time to look and sniff one out
Don hunting clothes, war paint, shaven legs
Washed hair, nails prepared
The right perfume to attract a mate
Who will be the lucky lad
Will he know I have need of his seed
For my clock to feed.

E Stirrup

ALONE

I open the door.
A sea of faces meet mine.
Angry eyes,
Burning hatred,
Willing me to step out of line.
The smallest thing, my life is over.
I'm sinking.
Sinking into a blur of darkness - alone.
Head spinning,
They're winning.
   Blank out their cruel taunts.
Words as sharp as knives, stabbing me over and over again.
Face flooding scarlet. Unbearable comments.
Tears are pricking in my eyes.
Which I must disguise.
Tears will only make it worse for me.
Confidence gone, panic erupting.
This is a dream that my brain is constructing.
It must be.
It isn't.
I snap back to reality with a jolt.
Sniggering invades my ears - my worst fears.
I am alone in this dangerous world of popularity.

The first blow hits me.
Searing pain, vision red,
Careless thoughts:
'I wish I was dead.'

Francesca Patel (13)

MARRIAGE, CHILDREN, DIVORCE

First Cycle - quarter century,
Several romances, wrong choices,
Taken for a ride again, then,
New man, new marriage.
Happy ever after? Big joke,
Unfaithful via the Internet,
Divorce again. Lessons learnt?
No, same idiot looking for love
And finding?
Same selfish manhood, serving self,
Treating women with contempt,
Fearing commitment.
Do we ever learn?

Gaynor Dack

WOMAN

The day comes, you're not a child now, but a woman,
And maturity and intuition come to you without summon.
A built-in force in you guides through feelings and emotions,
You see everybody differently and harbour secret devotions.
The reality of first love, the first kiss, like stepping off a ledge,
The feeling in your heart when you make your marriage pledge.
The flutter of a life inside, that first look into your new-born's eyes,
The businesswoman's success when reaching that for which she strives;
The nurturing of children, and ego's and ambitions,
That striving to bring everyone's hopes and dreams to fruition:
The wisdom gained throughout a life of work and dedication.
The essence of any woman, strong enough to run a nation.

Roseanna Tyrrell

EARTHBOUND SPIRIT

Angel of my dreams
        once you came to me
bound in the chains
        of your dark life.

Help me, you cried,
        release me from the bondage
of my unhappiness.
        Heal my tormented heart.

Deep compassion filled my soul
        and I wrapped him in my love.
Come with me, I said,
        I will take you to the light.

Let my spirit guide you
        let my love soothe your pain.
I will tell your story
        you have not lived in vain.

My dark angel wept and
        stretched out his trembling hands.
I took him in my arms
        and lifted him out of the night.

And he was folded in mystical wings
        he was bathed in golden light
as his spirit soared
        to other worldly realms.

Leaving me gazing
        at the starlit sky
endlessly searching
        endlessly waiting
for the dark angel
        who came to me one night.

Brigitta D'Arcy

MY LIFE

I need no man to hold my hand
though the days are long and the nights are lonely

       I am strong

When I toss and turn in the bed so cold
Who would be so bold to share the space

       I can be strong

When the tears roll from these eyes so tired
The cry so deep though I must hide the ache and sorrow

       I shall be strong

Who could I tell of the things now past
The pain and hurt and sordid deed

       I must be strong

The crumbled hope dragged from the heart
trampled in so young a frame
wisdom gained from hurt and pain
with whom could I share my life laid bare

       I have to be strong

I could not watch a tender look
turn to one of scorn
so I can never trust, to lay bare my life
I can never be a good man's wife.

       Please keep me strong.

Valerie Turner

CLEOPATRA

I am an asp
A slithering snake
Poisonous and venomous

I am Augustus
The first emperor of Rome
Son of Julius Caesar
Who fell in love with Cleopatra.

She was deposed after a coup
And restored to power

She lived in Egypt
After Caesar was assassinated
With lover Mark Anthony
A Roman politician.

Who committed suicide
After being defeated in battle
Cleopatra consented to a deathly bite
I charmed the rich beauty to death.

Ann Copland

TIME STOPPED

He said it with such pride,
Like a coy adolescent
Embarrassed by success,
He was gentle and calm.
'I've been seeing someone else'
Time stopped
Numb
Dumb
Petrified
My pen has stopped
No words to say
Because at that moment
My heart died.

Harriette Thomas

THESE HANDS

These hands tell a story of passing years
Of hardships and happiness, hopes and fears
Short and stubby and wrinkly today
No longer the young woman's hands of yesterday.

I remember the first occasion a boy held one tight
It opened up a new world of love and delight
But another hand held them and then a few more
Till finally they found what they were looking for.

The hands of the man with whom I chose to stay
Were caring and kind and are to this day
My hands have held his and loved him so dear
Fulfilled as a woman with him so near.

What a privilege holding my babies so soft and bare
My hardworking hands so rough to compare
The tasks they performed for these innocents so dear
Oh, the sweet memory of it all brings on a small tear.

I remember that time they held my Mum fast
If only they'd known it was to be their last
And now they stroke my dad as he lies in his bed
Trying to connect with the thoughts in his head.

My hands have done no more than any woman would do
And they're strong and yet useful after all they've been through
But they're a little uncertain now that middle age is here
Will they be valued and needed and keep their loved ones near?

A corner's been turned, there's no going back
These hands must continue, must follow the track
So much still to give, so much to learn
Help me, God, to make each day count, for years gone not to yearn.

J M Edwards

MEN!

I used to think I understood men
But many years have passed since then.
I've learned a lot along the way
And don't understand them at all today.
I used to think the way to their heart
Was via their stomach; and that's a fact
Which was told to women long ago.
Now I know it is just not so.
Many men say that they cannot talk,
But have you ever taken a walk
That leads you past an open pub door?
It's not silence emitting, that's for sure.
Men say that they do not complain
But they have no problem stating
What they don't like, or what to say
To put off a job to another day.
But I did not understand men
And though I've tried since then
All I have is an idea
That they're a complete enigma.

Louise McLennan

MUM

Although I never seem that grateful
For all the things you do
Whenever life seems difficult
I want to turn to you.

You taught me more than you'll ever know
And made my life worth living
By protecting me from danger
With the love you keep on giving.

I know that I can count on you
Through my laughter and my tears
Whatever happens in my life
You can ease my fears.

I really want to tell you
You inspire everything I do
You've worked hard to give me all you could
And I am truly thankful to you.

So for every minute of every day
This is what I want to say
Although we've had problems through the years
I continue to love you in every way.

Christina Northfield

A DREAM OF THE FUTURE

Our colour and creed
Should not breed

Hatred or violence
Intolerance and silence.

Freedom and justice
Belong to us all.

Because we're God's children
After all.

I have a dream
Both sides of the tracks.

Can sit down together
Not turn their backs.

I have a dream.

Jacquie Seales

WOMAN EMERGING

The void. That devouring fog of intruded dignity -
Where exploded truths of a wastrel
With sweet-smelling complexion,
Warm, honeyed contentment
And paraphrased murmur of clichés -
Quivered emotions
To the bondage of trembling euphoria.

Woodsmoke and crystal and gentle awakening
Splashed with the brilliance of headlights
All rubies and diamonds on darkest black velvet
And silver-blue eyes, a swirl to the dancing
Of waltzes and dreams and of golden-corn lies.

Ambitious woman who
Gyrated to the fluctuations of his
Smart atavistic and slick
Manipulated stock,
A business man with no profitless deals who
Contemptuously flourished a future
With the goose-quilled pen
Now urged to tears on a grandiose scale
As she disintegrates to shadows
With no splinter of light.

No!
No fractured symmetry and no still-life,
No burnt fingers the match can drop.
No stunted trees, bogeymen and no audible agony
Just sweet-dappled sunlight of every tomorrow's
Coolest glades
Stride lengthened, lights flashing, surging forward, soaring
Nobody will impede the destiny of woman.

Robyn Dalby

REVEALED EMOTIONS

Courageous
Like a warrior
Yet frightened,
Like an animal running from its predator.
Togetherness.
Like a close family,
Yet loneliness,
Like an orphan.
Joyfulness
Like a newly wed couple
Yet sadness,
Like a widow
Comfort,
Like dreaming in a deep sleep,
Yet pain
Like a bullet in the head.
Appreciated
Like a nurse,
Yet worthless,
Like a tramp.
Free,
Like a bird in the wild,
Yet trapped,
Like a prisoner in a cell.
Love,
Like a father gives to his son,
Yet hatred,
Like a Nazi gave to a Jew,

Calm,
Like the sea on a summer's day,
Yet anger,
Like a volcano ready to erupt,
Talented,
Like Picasso or Monet,
Yet incompetent
Like a child learning how to write.

This is how I feel
These are my revealed emotions.

Wendy Funston

ADULT EDUCATION

A young single mother
Turns to no other
To care for her son
She does it alone.

Another young woman
In the grip of depression
Slashes up her arm
They call it self harm.

Another girl loses her grandmother
Her father does all he can to smother
Her feelings of grief
Till she is left to seethe.

Trapped in a disease ridden skin
Another keeps within
Her feelings of anger
Toward her drunken mother.

Feeling a little too tall
Another thinks she should be small
And hears laughter from folk
She thinks find her a joke.

She is not alone
Another's paranoia has grown
To the sort of proportion
That makes even good friends show caution.

With you a secret I shall trust
For tell it I must
All of these six women
I met doing adult education.

These women I admire
To have their strength I would aspire.

Gill Drake

THE BOUNTY

She gently cradled his head,
His clammy brow pressed against her chest,
A tender stroke across his cheek,
A silent whisper echoing in his ear.

The sharp red pain,
Shooting through the body's core,
Tearing flesh and bone apart,
Inner screams caught amidst.

And finally when all is done,
She wipes his tears and forms a smile.
Triumphantly tired and still,
She passes him the bounty child.

Joanne McGuinness

PEACE POEM

What is peace?
Peace is when people live together.
Live together without fighting or being at war
And when we all treat each other equally
And do not care about skin colour or what religion we are.

Sadly today we still have not achieved peace.
Not even in our own small country.
But we are trying to light that light.
The light of peace that will bring brightness to the whole world.
We are so close but yet so far away from it.

We, the future, must play our part in the future of peace
However small it may seem.
We must learn to now trust and respect our fellow man.
And try to put behind us the injustice and oppression of the past.
And look forward to a future full of freedom and justice.
We must try harder to light that light.

Sarah Scott

BULLYING

You just can't run,
You just can't hide,
All that pain locked up inside.
You don't know just
What to do,
The sorrows
Pelting down on you.
The fear is tearing
You apart,
It's been like that right from the start,
You want to cry,
You can't tell anyone -
You'd rather die!
On your own - it won't go away,
Just speak up - you've got something to say.
Don't let bullying get you down,
You've got a chance - don't turn it down.

Amy Rogers-Newnham

INNOCENCE

A child, a hope
A new beginning
An innocent start
No hidden past
No secrets within
A new star at night
A new beginning
An innocent start
A guiding light
To a whole new world
Still works its magic
In the beholder's eye
Leading to a new dimension
A wise man to an infant king.

Jenny Johnston

THE SPACE WE SHARE

People all around me
Like mad as hatter hares
All having tons of fun
In the space we share.

A feeling of tranquillity
Love, peace, care,
All these feelings around me,
In the space we share.

I love to be in this place
Earth is what it's called.
The sun, the moon, the stars, the air,
In the space we share.

Not one or two or three spaces
The whole earth, I crave.
It's the place I love to be
And is the space we share.

Christina Kennedy

FATIGUE

Disillusioned and tired
Work with such little time
Little, just enough.
Exactly planned to the frantic minute
Assuredly stumbling into pre-ordained places
Vibrant frustration with obvious weaknesses
Helpless self-assurance.

Johanna Wilson

UPS AND DOWN OF LIFE

Joy of joy, I've grown at last
Oh no it's up and out too fast.
I like the style the fashions simple.
Just look at my chin, I've got a pimple.

I'd like nice legs all long and slender.
I'd wear big shoes but my feet are tender.
I'd dye my hair and have it curly,
Oh no it's like a curly wurly.

I love the way I'm in my teens,
But it's strange to have these crazy genes.
I want to be so chic and cool.
Does this purple hair make me look a fool.

Dale Maginnes

SHOPPING BLISS - THE SALES WE SHARE

My heaven stays open from nine till five,
In there you have to fight to stay alive,
It's all very well, browsing through the rails,
But it turns into murder in the January sales.

Rushing from the top, that's only a fiver,
Running out of changing rooms, like Lady Godiva.
Getting great deals, hardly spending a penny,
But come in too late and you just won't get any.

Buying things that maybe don't fit you quite right,
But for less than a tenner who cares if they're tight.
Go into designer shops but hey, let's be frank,
For that sort of stuff you'd have to rob a bank.

You go through the fighting to stay in the trend,
But always it's worth it, truly my friend.
Yeah at the start there'll be screams, tears and cries.
But then you go home and swoon over your buys.

Claire Long

MOTHER AND CHILD

Everyone has felt this connection once.
Sharing everything with their mother.
What she hears, you hear.
What she eats, you eat.
What she fears, you fear.
You share her hands, her eyes, her feet.

She gives up her life.
But she doesn't care.
Only one thing matters to her.
The place the two of you share.

Her body is yours
Till the day you are born.
But on this day, I'm sad to say.
The link is sometimes torn.

Christine Long

SHYLOCK DEVIL

Getting compassion for this heartless man
was like killing the wind in a terrible storm
he sat and rocked in his chair
not causing any harm
but he lived down low beside the fire
this man was a heartless liar
man or beast he may be
none can describe what they did not see.

Tracy Knox

A Space We Need To Share - Bullying

A new school year and all was well,
I'd settled in just fine.
No longer in the infant school
The junior class was mine.
I made new friends, I loved the work
I felt mature and smart,
But little did I know that soon
My world would fall apart.

Our table had three girls plus me,
And one was my best friend.
At first we all got on quite well
But that was soon to end.
The other two ganged up on me
And made my life so hard.
They whispered, laughed and stared at me
And I felt such a coward.

I was so much afraid of them
Because of things they'd do.
They'd steal my break and hide my books
Make playtime torture too.
I couldn't eat and couldn't sleep
And hated going to school,
I wouldn't tell my mum and dad
That wouldn't have been 'cool'.

I realised I'd have to tell
Because things were so bad
So one day I burst into tears
And told my mum and dad.
They were a bit annoyed, because
I'd took so long to tell,
So next day Mum went up to school
Before the first school bell.

At last it was all sorted out
The teacher helped a lot
He lectured us on 'Bullying'
And said it had to stop.
'Please do not suffer like I did
And take a tip from me
Don't bottle it up inside yourself
Tell someone and be free!'

Jenny McGarvey

ARE WE ANTS?

Ants,
black ants,
thousands of them,
scurrying around in their new black coats.
So many, I am just one of them.
One in a thousand.
Inside wasn't so bad.
I met a young lady called Miss Irwin.
She was called a teacher.
My teacher.
I played all day with the ants,
they're quite nice really,
when you get to know them.
I moved up through the years
and I remember vaguely
a wedding of my brother's,
where I was bridesmaid.
I was nine then,
five years after my first day at school.
On that day, the day of the wedding
there were no blank ants,
just lots of people, dressed colourfully,
all smiling and saying how cute I was.
Then there was another wedding.
My sister's turn this time.
More colourful smiley people.
And a new school.
Primary School was over now,
Time to grow up,
Glenlola this time
No blank ants now,
Just a thousand blue people.

Looking to the future
What will happen then?
I know what I want
But it's all just dreams.
I want to leave school
And go to University.
Marriage
Kids
Family
And a house.
A life in America
And become a famous journalist.
Will it really happen
Or is it just a dream?

Julie Loyal

MILLENNIUM

As I look back over the years,
I remember all the important things,
That have taken place in my life.
All the sadness, joy, laughter and anger.
Have helped to develop me into what I am today.
Learning to ride my bike, hitting double figures.
Filled me with joy and laughter.
But losing members of my family,
Made me cry with sadness.
Passing all my exams,
Made me feel happy and relaxed.
All this helped me on my journey of life.

As for the future, nobody can say,
But I hope that one day
I will achieve my goal
And become an interior designer.
I hopefully will be a wife to a rich man
And own a huge house and sporty car,
I'd like to have two kids,
Three dogs and one cat.
I could open my own business
And decorate people's houses.
But no one knows what will happen
So all I can do is hope.

Rebekah Lunn

WAVES CRASH IN

As I sit here, alone at the seashore
Everything around me - I ignore,
Rain falls down on me,
As though I am being punished.
So many memories fill me with dread,
So many things left unsaid.

The waves crash in
And the waves sweep out.
My life - what is it all about?
Sitting here alone, this mass of
Blues and greens.
I feel so insignificant
None understands what I mean.

Gemma McAleer

THIS ISLAND WE SHARE

In the past
there were bombings and terror
pain and sadness
death and murder.
We have suffered so much
but for what?
Hundreds of people have died
for no reason.
Fighting isn't solving anything.

The future reveals itself
as a time for change
a new beginning
a time to wipe the slates clean.
A time to forget about the past hardships and troubles
to blank out the bombings and terror.
A time for peace!

Allie McAuley

MY ROCKS

A thousand miles,
a million years
I want to be nowhere,
but at my beach,
my friends and I,
all alone,
watching the waves as they come.

It's nothing special,
to anyone but me,
sitting on the rocks,
watching the glistening sea,
the sun sometimes comes,
to keep us company,
but still it's mine
no need to watch the time.

A thousand miles,
I've been and back,
but still I want to be nowhere,
but at my beach.

Jane McDowell

MERRY MILLENNIUM

I hope the future holds better times
This past year has held tears, disappointments and a few laughs
For our community and as well for the whole country
There has been the Good Friday agreement
Many peace talks
But it has also seen things
Like the Omagh bomb and
Many serious punishment beatings.
I hope the year 2000
Will hold peace for Northern Ireland
Which would be some consolation
For all those people who have lost friends
Or relatives in 'The Troubles!'
I hope it would also bring
A few personal successes
So Merry Millennium.

Jenny McIlhatton

A DAY IN THE SUN

Feeling the steady, rolling movements of the horse beneath me
I am alive and free,
Boundless valleys and hills stretch before me.
I scrunch my eyes and look at the horizon
And wonder where to go, pretending I don't know
Where home is, so I won't have to go there.
I wake my horse up and sensing my burst of energy
She suddenly springs into canter and charges down the hill
In pursuit of something only known to herself.
I let her
I let the warm air turn cold and rush around me
As we head down the hill
I enjoy the exhilaration of the flight
And when we finally slow down when
The horse forgets why she's running
I grudgingly give in to responsibility
And head for home,
My day in the sun over.

Hayley Kirkpatrick

SLEDGING

Plastic bags
Baby baths
Frisbees
And lots of laughs.

People sledging on the snow
Shouting
Seeing how far they can go
Sledging on the snow.

Dads are pulling
Mums are worrying
Kids are laughing.

Naomi Pollock

WORLD CITIZENSHIP PROJECT

We are greedy for power
It is our light in a dark tunnel
We are enemies amongst each other
We are keen to criticise
But not so keen to be criticised ourselves.
Don't you see what we have become?
Think how you would feel if you were made fun of,
The reason, how you look.
It doesn't change who you are,
Or what you should or shouldn't be able to do.
Here in Northern Ireland
We have reached an agreement to stop fighting,
And promote peace.
You all could do the same
Come together and be friends
It could change the way the world is now.
Just stop fighting
And get on leading a happy life.

Kayleigh Richardson

WHO ARE WE TO JUDGE

I have found through my life
That peace does not come easily.
Lots of people care
About the world their children grow up
In and their safety.
Others don't care at all.
Whether it is peace between a mother and son
Or between politicians
It should be sorted out.
Not by fights or wars
But by agreement.
What is the point of fighting?
What do you gain from it?
I'll tell you, nothing
Nothing but guilt.
Just because we are different colours
Or better off than others.
We should still have rights
Anyway, who are we to judge?
Nobody is perfect.
So for a new millennium.
Should be a new future,
A path filled with joy.

Laura Robinson

HILLS AND VALLEYS

Hills and valleys
Like rolling waves of the sea.
Remind me of my life.
The love and hate for it seems to
Even each other out.
My heart jumps when I remember the
Good times.
This seems to overcome the silence
Of the land.
The sorrow and heartache it takes me to,
The dark sky above hangs over me in
Times of sadness.
But turns blue when times get better.
In the distance I see the horizon
Behind more rough hills and valleys.
Reminding me of the good and bad
Times that still have to come.

Stephanie Haslett

UNTITLED

Taken for granted,
Yet always there,
Without it, what would happen?
Finally, its importance realised?

It has a lot to do,
Every morning it must rise.
To let the world wake up
And open up its eyes.

It lets things grow
It keeps things warm,
It lets us exist,
Still it's taken for granted.

Without it the world would perish.
And would be plunged;
Into a pool of darkness,
And the cold would seize,
The once warm atmosphere,
And kill everything;
Which depends on it.
Any life would cease to exist,
Yet, still it is taken for granted.

Caragh Geddis

THE TRAPPED WORLD

Shadow lining the eyes
Darkness engulfing the brain
Calming the thoughts
Dimming the lights
A fantasy light shines into the mind
Revealing beautiful land
Strange birds fly through the air
So fresh and alive
Momentary darkness
The dragon flies past the sun
He blows a fire of fear
The light disappears
This time it doesn't come back
Shadow and darkness engulf the land
The fantasies have gone
Locked in darkness
Wanting to escape
But they can't get through the shadow lining.

Lynne Emerson

WHO CAN HELP?

I saw her standing every day
Alone and deadly white
She wouldn't tell me what was wrong
Or how to make it right.

She never seemed to have a friend
She always sat alone
Most girls just passed her by
But some would stop to moan.

They called her names and hid her bag
They kicked her lunch box out the door
I couldn't see the joy they got
When all her pens fell on the floor.

They wrote some lies upon her locker
I knew it wasn't right
I saw the pain that she was in
But still she wouldn't fight.

At last the teacher saw her cry
And tried to help her find
A friend to share her troubles with
But I couldn't, it would be a bind!

Kerry Savage

THE HIDDEN ME

Why can't I say what I think?
My mind bursting with feelings,
Exploding with the most heartfelt emotion.
My thoughts, however abundant, are hidden within.
I am the person you never will see,
I am the dark, shrouded being
That camouflages itself in human skin.

I don't know what I want from life,
Or why I feel this abysmal anger.
It manifests inside me like a menacing mould,
Never-ending torment, driving me wild, insane.

Does anyone hear my thoughts?
Or am I alone in this isolation?
The cave of darkness that entraps me.
Is it empty but for my soul?
Or can any other feel my pain?
I crave for an answer but no one can hear,
I search for the exit, driven by fear.
My efforts are worthless, why bother to try?
When only I can hear, why bother to cry?

Lyndsey Cunningham

A SHADOW

A shadow now lay over the valley
A blanket for the night, for the dead.

He straightens up his bent back
Leans on his stick, and begins,
Begins to walk along the country road.

Every night the stones crunching below his old tattered shoes.
A lonely man in search of her and where he finds her lying is tragic
Beyond a grey wall rising high above him.

With gates locked strong,
Why?
To keep her in or him out.
She appears to him on her perch
Motionless.

He longs for his gates to open
So that he will be with her
But they won't let him in, not yet, not now.

Kelly Gallagher

MY CHILD

My child though we stand in defeat
And our nation all divided and fallen now weeps
And many of our population lay scattered where killed
Though we have journeyed afar by feet
And know not where lies the cruel hands of our fate
We shall trail on into the oppressive night and late
Travelling over mountains and hills
Searching again for soils that grow and reap
Where sirens of danger do not raise our fears with their drills
Where our extinguished race awakes from the dead of their sleep
Where our homes are not derelict but again with life filled
Where we are not demoralised in queues where we await
With faces covered in tears of anguish and hate
Savaged upon by beasts like bait
So my child with strength and courage your heart fill
For in our search if I am to grow weary and die
Do not stop in a serge of blighted sorrow and weep
Continue until the vision in your eyes is fulfilled
Recapture our homeland where we so much suffered
Rise with your generation and avenge every other
Who brought us with bullets to our knees
Who infected our dwellings that were once so harmonic and sweet
Burning our beautiful fields that once swayed in ripe wheat
And most of all my child heal our great nation that constantly bleeds

Saheeda Khan

SUBMISSIONS INVITED
SOMETHING FOR EVERYONE

WOMENSWORDS 2001 - Strictly women,
have your say the female way!

POETRY NOW 2001 - Any subject,
any style, any time.

STRONGWORDS 2001 - Warning!
Age restriction, must be between 16-24,
opinionated and have strong views.
(Not for the faint-hearted)

All poems no longer than 30 lines.
Always welcome! No fee!
Cash Prizes to be won!

Mark your envelope (eg Poetry Now) *2001*
Send to: Forward Press Ltd
Remus House, Coltsfoot Drive,
Peterborough, PE2 9JX

**OVER £10,000 POETRY PRIZES
TO BE WON!**
Judging will take place in October 2001